TRADITIONAL COUNTRY LIFE RECIPE SERIES

FRESH HERB COMPANION

TRADITIONAL COUNTRY LIFE RECIPE SERIES

FRESH HERB COMPANION

Jane Wilson Morton
&
Marianne K. Preston

Cover Illustration
Lisa Adams

The Brick Tower Press ™
1230 Park Avenue, New York, NY 10128

Printed in the United States by J. T. Colby & Company, Inc., New York.

Morton, Jane Wilson
Preston, Marianne K.
The Traditional Country Life Recipe Series:
Fresh Herb Companion -- 1st Edition
Includes Index
ISBN 1-883283-04-3 softcover

Library of Congress Catalog Card
Number: 93-74031
September 1994
First Edition

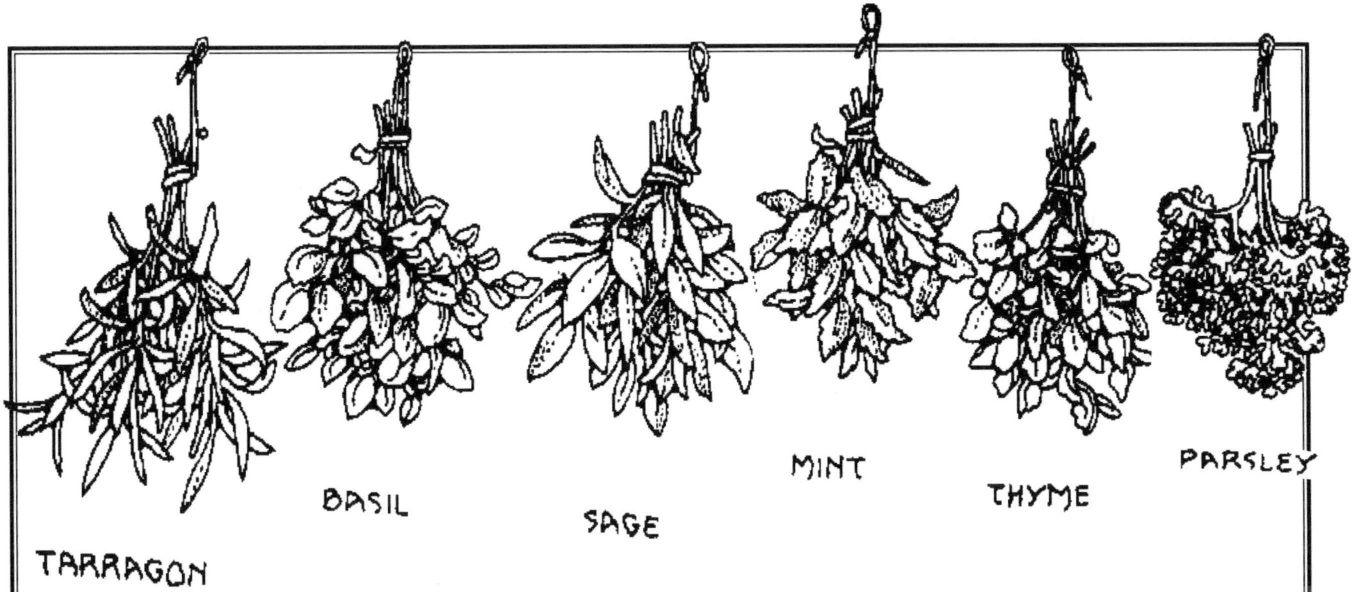

INTRODUCTION

Herbs are the jewels in the crown of the simplest as well as the most complicated recipes. As we all search for the most natural way to enhance the flavor of a main ingredient and still follow the guidelines for a well-balanced diet, it is herbs that come to the rescue. With their variety of flavors the cook can cut back on salt and fats and easily fall into line with the suggestions of nutrition and health professionals.

In general, herbs grow in temperate climates and the flavor oils reside in the leaves of the plants. Spices come from tropical climes and are the root, bark, seed, berries, and buds of various plants and trees. Herbs and spices are

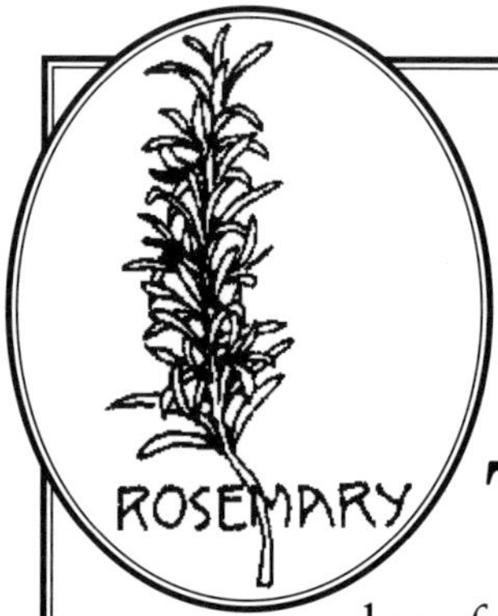

frequently used together. Mixtures like chili powder and curry powder are a combination of spices and herbs. There is a recipe for making your own Chili Powder on page 5. Try it!

This collection of recipes uses commonly grown and easily accessible garden herbs found throughout American folklore from the Pilgrims to modern times. In 1796, Amelia Simmons wrote, in the First American Cookbook, "Garlicks, tho' used by the French, are better adapted to the use of medicine than cooking." How tastes have changed in 200 years! Simmons also designated "the seven herbs useful in cookery" as thyme, sweet marjoram, savory, sage, parsley, pennyroyal, and horseradish. All but pennyroyal are still popular.

Herbs have a worldly heritage that includes the renowned "herbs of Provence" - rosemary, thyme, and tarragon - the heart and soul of French provincial and Mediterranean cooking. Sesame (benne) seeds came to the Americas through the African slave trade and we enjoy them regularly on cookies, cakes, and bagels. Meanwhile, travelers to the Americas took indigenous American seasonings, like allspice berries, and sweet and hot peppers, back to their native lands.

Cilantro, alias coriander and Chinese parsley, seasons foods in the American southwest, as well as in Mexico, China, and India. Basil, one of our favorites, came into widespread use in the United States after World War II when American servicemen brought it home from Europe. Now it's a mainstay on American herb shelves, and is almost as available as parsley in the supermarket produce department.

An herb garden is a sensory garden. You rub the leaves and sniff the fragrance on your fingertips. You pinch a leaf and nibble to test the strength of the flavor. Seeing, touching, smelling, tasting; these are the senses that are stimulated as you bring an herb garden to fruition. Touch the savory, enjoy the aroma of mint and basil, and appreciate the delicate flavor of woodruff.

Our cookbook provides the cook with a delightful array of sensate recipes - from beverages, appetizers, and breads, to soups, vegetables, and desserts. A recipe like Cornmeal Madeleines with Chives and Jalapenos combines the native American ingredients, corn and jalapeno pepper, to produce southwestern flavor in the shape of a famous French tea cake. Bread Pudding with herbs and fruit still uses day-old bread but takes a new twist when you add oregano, thyme, mint, and a touch of cayenne pepper. Soft Custard, long a standby as a nutritious dessert for children or a recuperating patient, is imbued with a touch of elegance when subtly flavored with bay leaf.

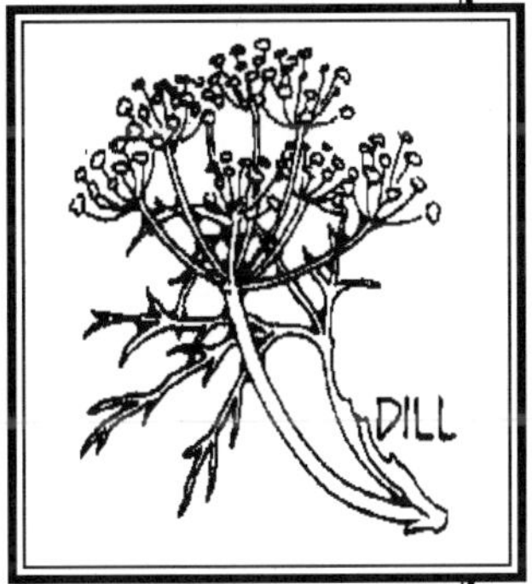

Herbs play various roles in the makeup of a recipe. They can be subtle enhancers that lay back and give the main ingredient the lead role, as in Lemon Verbena Chicken Wings or Basic Chicken Soup. They can be the dominant flavor that maintains its own identity but blends with the main ingredient as in Roast Leg of Lamb with Garlic and Oregano or Herb Garden Potato Salad. Or, they can take over entirely and be the BIG taste of the recipe as in Pesto Sauce or Cajun Mayonnaise.

As we approach the twenty-first century, herbs have a new persona with their inclusion in dessert recipes, as both flavoring and garnish. Peek at the recipes for Fruit Kuchen or Coriander and Apricot Cake. Each uses an herb in an innovative way to add a new dimension to old American standards. For garnishing a dessert, try a sprig of thyme or sage, a shiny bay leaf or a colorful nasturtium blossom.

We hope that each recipe you try entices you to try another and yet another. Perhaps you will be inspired to plant a few herbs or expand a present herb bed. You will start to think differently about flavoring your foods and be on your way to new culinary adventures. Let your taste buds be your major guide. Substitute one herb for another and experiment. Herbs, with their flavor and beauty, whether they come from the home garden, the greengrocer, or the supermarket, provide pleasure to the eye, nose, mind, and palate.

JANE WILSON MORTON & MARIANNE K. PRESTON
New York, 1994

CHIVES

TABLE OF CONTENTS

HERBAL HINTS

1 Good kitchen shears are the best utensil for gathering herbs from the garden as well as for snipping them into small pieces.

2 Use a less pungent herb seasoning for a weak flavored main ingredient in order to achieve a happy flavor balance.

3 If you're not sure of an herb's specific flavor, mix some with unsalted butter, let it stand for an hour, then spread on a plain cracker and taste.

4 To substitute dried herbs for fresh, use half the quantity called for in the recipe.

5 Coarse or woody stems of herbs should be discarded when chopping the leaves. Young, tender stems can be included.

6 To strip small leaves off stems (e.g. thyme), hold the sprig by the tender end and gently run your fingers along the stem toward the tough root end, pushing the leaves off as you go. The tender tip will break off and can be used.

7 Gather the herbs needed for the day early in the morning, when they are freshest. Rinse with cool water to clean, and stand stems in a glass of cold water until ready to use.

8 Basil leaves or other large leafy herbs, used in salad or as garnish, are best torn into pieces with the fingers to prevent discoloring.

9 To "chiffonade" large leaves like basil, stack several leaves one on top of the other, lay them on a board in front of you with the length of the leaves running left to right. Roll them into a tight cylinder and slice as thinly as you possibly can. You will have fine little shreds of basil.

10 The flowers of herbs are edible and make charming garnishes. Chive flowers can be used whole when garnishing or torn apart and scattered into a salad.

11 Almost all herbs make interesting teas. Mint, lemon verbena, thyme, sage, and bee balm (bergamot) are some you can use. Bergamot is a native American herb introduced to settlers by the Oswego Indians. Tea made from the leaves is called Oswego Tea. 2 teaspoons of crushed fresh herb steeped in 1 cup of boiling water for 5-10 minutes will produce a nice tea. Strain out the herbs.

12 Herb infused vinegars and oils are popular. Add herbs to warmed vinegar or oil, bottle and let sit for a couple of weeks, then enjoy their new flavor. Tarragon is one of the more popular herb vinegars, and a stalk of crushed lemon grass gives a subtle taste to oil or vinegar.

13 Maximum flavor is extracted when you add herbs to a sauté pan as you heat the oil or butter. For long, slow cooking, add herbs during the last 30 minutes of simmering.

14 Bay leaves are indigestible and should be removed before a dish is served.

15 The flavor of herb seeds like coriander, mustard, cumin, fennel, and sesame intensify if heated in a 300° F. oven for 3-5 minutes or in a non-stick skillet for 2-3 minutes. The same is true of nuts.

16 Drying herbs:

The easiest method is to wash and dry a few stalks of the herb, tie them together at the stem end, and hang upside down in a dry, warm spot with good air circulation, out of direct sun.

OR

Wash and dry the herbs, strip the large leaves off the stems, dry the smaller stems whole. Spread out on a piece of screening where air can circulate on all sides freely. It takes about a week for them to dry. Turn the leaves regularly during the process.

OR

Microwave - check your microwave book for the best approach for your particular model.

OR

Oven method - spread clean leaves on a baking tray and place in a 200° F. oven for about 20 minutes or more. The dried herbs should retain some of their green color and be completely dry. Cool and place into clean jars. Cap, label, and store in a cool, dark, dry place.

17 Dried herbs maintain peak flavor for about 6 months so gauge your purchases according to the quantity you regularly use.

18 "Fines Herbes" are a blend of parsley, chervil, chives, and tarragon.

19 "Bouquet Garni" includes bay leaf, parsley, and thyme. The herbs may be tied in a little cheesecloth packet - OR you can use the parsley stem to tie around the bay leaf and thyme - OR you can place the herbs into the hollow of a 3-inch piece of outer stalk of celery, cover with a second piece, and tie them together. This technique allows the flavor of the herbs to permeate the soup or stew while providing a way to discard the herbs easily when you wish.

20 Barbecue Blend includes cumin, garlic, hot pepper, and oregano.

21 Remember that you must be the ultimate judge of how much seasoning you want in a particular dish. Start with a small amount, taste, add more if desired.

22 CHILI POWDER - 1 teaspoon of cayenne pepper, 3 teaspoons of sweet paprika, 1 teaspoon of cumin powder, 1 teaspoon of ground coriander, 1/2 teaspoon of Mexican oregano, 1/4 teaspoon of allspice, a pinch of cloves. Combine all ingredients, mixing well. Store in a cool place, in an airtight jar. (The freezer and refrigerator are excellent for storage).

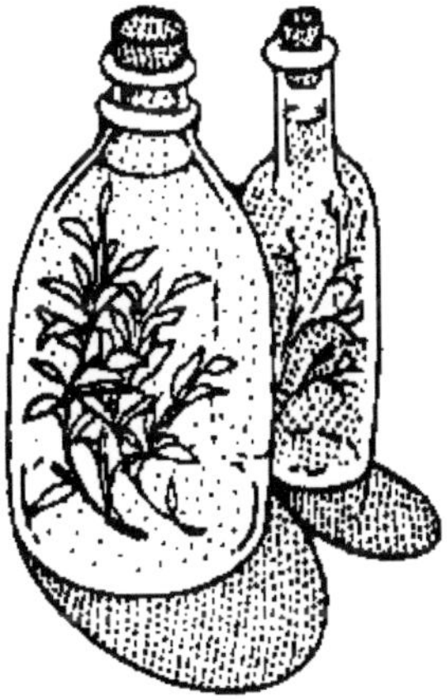

COTTAGE CHEESE WITH HERBS

(1) In a medium bowl, combine the cottage cheese, tarragon, parsley, thyme, onion chives, black pepper, and cayenne pepper.
(2) Cover and chill for 3 or 4 hours or up to 3 days.
(3) Place in a serving dish; sprinkle with paprika and garnish with a chive blossom, nasturtium, or parsley sprig in the center.
(4) Serve with cut vegetables or triangles of toasted bread or crackers.

INGREDIENTS

2 cups of cottage cheese
1 tablespoon of minced tarragon
1 tablespoon of minced flat leaf parsley
1 teaspoon of minced thyme
1 tablespoon of minced onion chives
1/2 teaspoon of coarsely ground black pepper
1/8 teaspoon of cayenne pepper (optional)
1/4 teaspoon of paprika
1 chive blossom, nasturtium, or parsley sprig

MAKES 2 1/4 CUPS

OREGANO AND PARMESAN
TOAST CRISPS

Preheat oven to 350° F.

(1) Quarter the loaf of bread and cut into 1/2-inch slices.
(2) Toast the bread on both sides in a toaster or under a broiler.
(3) Place the toasted slices on a baking tray.
(4) Combine oregano, two cheeses, and olive oil.
(5) Spoon the cheese mix onto the bread, making sure the surface of the bread is covered.
(6) Sprinkle on cayenne pepper.
(7) Bake for 15 minutes in preheated oven or until cheese is crusty and golden.
(8) Cool and store in tins until ready to serve.

INGREDIENTS

1 round loaf of crusty bread
1 cup of minced oregano leaves
1 1/2 cups of shredded Parmesan cheese
1/2 cup of shredded, sharp cheddar cheese
1/8 cup of olive oil
cayenne pepper (optional)

NOTE: *These will hold for up to 2 weeks in a cool place. To increase the yield to 40 pieces cut each slice in half. Serve with cocktails, salads, or omelets.*

MAKES ABOUT 20 SLICES

HAM, CHEESE 'N CHIVE
PINWHEELS

(1) Blend the two cheeses together.
(2) Add the chives and dillweed; blend well.
(3) Lay a slice of ham on a cutting board. Trim to even its shape, if necessary. Spread 1/4 of the cheese mixture evenly over the entire slice, covering all edges.
(4) Roll up the ham from the short end, snugly.
(5) Repeat this process with the remaining 3 slices of ham.
(6) Place the four rolls on a plate, cover with plastic wrap and refrigerate for 2 hours or overnight.
(7) When ready to serve, slice rolls into 1/4 inch slices. Serve the pinwheels on crackers or by themselves with toothpicks.

NOTE: *The rolls will keep in the refrigerator for a week.*

INGREDIENTS

4 ounces of light cream cheese, at room temperature
2 ounces of blue cheese or gorgonzola, at room temperature
2 tablespoons of snipped chives
1 tablespoon of freshly snipped dillweed
4 thin slices of delicatessen Virginia baked ham

MAKES 48 PINWHEELS

LEMON VERBENA CHICKEN WINGS

Preheat oven to 350° F.

(1) Snip off wing tips and discard or use for chicken soup (see page 16).
(2) Cut remaining wings into two pieces at the joint; place in a baking dish. Sprinkle with the garlic.
(3) Bake in a preheated oven for 30 minutes, turning once or twice.
(4) In a small bowl whisk together olive oil, verbena, 1/3 cup of chives, lemon juice, salt, and both peppers.
(5) When wings have baked for 30 minutes, coat them with the oil mixture.
(6) Bake until golden and crisp, about 30 more minutes.
(7) Transfer to a serving dish.
(8) Discard oil from baking dish; scrape drippings over the wings.
(9) Arrange the blossoms and sprigs of lemon verbena attractively on top.

INGREDIENTS

24 chicken wings
2 large cloves of garlic, minced
1/2 cup of olive oil
1/2 cup of minced lemon verbena
1/3 cup of minced garlic chives
1/8 cup of fresh lemon juice
1 teaspoon of salt
1 teaspoon of black pepper
1/8 teaspoon of cayenne pepper
6 garlic chive blossoms
sprigs of lemon verbena

NOTE: *Regular chives may be substituted for garlic chives.*

MAKES 48 PIECES

MUSSELS WITH CILANTRO

(1) In a small saucepan heat the scallions, soy sauce, sugar, ginger, and lemon juice.
(2) Arrange the mussels in their shells on an attractive tray.
(3) Pour the warm sauce over all. Sprinkle with cilantro and red pepper.
(4) Serve at room temperature.

INGREDIENTS

1 bunch scallions, with tops, minced
1/2 cup of light soy sauce
1 teaspoon of sugar
1 tablespoon of minced ginger
juice of 1 small lemon
3 pounds of mussels, cooked and left on the half shell
1/2 cup of chopped fresh cilantro
1/4 cup of minced red pepper

SERVES 4

SAVORY SALMON SPREAD

(1) Drain salmon, reserving 2 teaspoons of liquid; flake.
(2) Combine cream cheese, lemon basil, or lemon verbena, scallions, parsley, liquid smoke, and reserved liquid. Blend thoroughly.
(3) Fold in flaked salmon.
(4) Pack into a suitable bowl, cover, and chill for several hours or overnight. Garnish with nasturtium and serve with whole wheat herb seed crackers (see page 70).

INGREDIENTS

7 1/2 ounces of canned Alaska salmon
8 ounces of cream cheese, softened
1 tablespoon of finely minced lemon basil or lemon verbena
3 tablespoons of minced scallions
2 tablespoons of minced parsley
3 drops of liquid smoke flavoring
1 nasturtium flower

SERVES 6-8

SOUTHWESTERN TOMATO DIP

(1) Heat olive oil in a large sauté pan.
(2) Add the onion, garlic, oregano, cilantro, cumin seeds, salt, and sugar. Combine and simmer 5 minutes.
(3) Add 1/2 cup of tomato and sauté on high for 5 minutes. Add the remaining tomatoes in 1/2 cup portions sautéing each addition for 5 minutes.
(4) Lower the heat; cook uncovered, for 10 minutes. Stir frequently.
(5) Remove from the heat and cool.
(6) Reseason to your taste with salt, add pepper, and extra sugar if the tomatoes seem tart. Transfer to a ceramic or stainless steel bowl.
(7) Cover. Store in refrigerator for at least 24 hours before serving.
(8) To serve, transfer to a serving bowl and use as a dip for corn chips or vegetables or as a sauce for grilled chicken or omelets.

INGREDIENTS

3 tablespoons of olive oil
1 cup of diced onion
1 large clove of garlic, minced
1 tablespoon of minced oregano leaves
1 tablespoon of minced cilantro leaves
1 tablespoon of crushed cumin seeds
1 teaspoon of salt
1 teaspoon of sugar
3 cups of tomatoes, peeled and chopped
1 teaspoon of pepper

NOTE: *See note on page 19 for peeling tomatoes.*

MAKES 1 1/2 CUPS

YELLOW AND RED ROASTED PEPPERS
WITH HERB DRESSING

(1) Roast peppers under broiler or on the barbecue until the skin is black all around; about 15 minutes. Cool and peel off the blackened skin under running water.
(2) While peppers are roasting, warm olive oil and add 1 sprig each of the thyme and savory. Set Aside.
(3) Remove the pepper stems by carefully pulling, removing as much of the seeded core as possible. Cut each pepper into four sections, remove any remaining seeds and ribs and lay the pieces out flat on a platter.
(4) Strip the leaves from the remaining thyme and savory stems; chop fine.
(5) Tuck garlic slices between pepper quarters.
(6) Sprinkle the prepared herbed oil, vinegar, and minced herbs over the pepper pieces. Let marinate at room temperature at least 1 hour.
(7) To serve, cut peppers and cheese to fit on crackers. Garnish with thyme or savory.

INGREDIENTS

2 sweet red peppers, unblemished, evenly shaped
2 sweet yellow peppers, unblemished, evenly shaped
1/4 cup of extra-virgin olive oil
3 sprigs of thyme, about 3-inches long
3 sprigs of winter savory, about 3-inches long
1 or 2 cloves of garlic, peeled and sliced thin
1 tablespoon of red or sherry wine vinegar
4 or 6 slices of mozzarella or feta cheese

NOTE: *To serve as a salad, place red and yellow pepper quarters on a bed of greens. Add cheese slices. Drizzle with some of the dressing from the peppers. Garnish.*

SERVES 4-6

GLORIOUS
AMERICAN ANTIPASTO

(1) Place each ingredient in a separate bowl except the anchovies, greens, vinegar, oil, parsley, and basil. Cut large artichokes in half.

(2) Line a large round or oval platter with the greens.

(3) Start layering the various ingredients, sprinkling a few pieces of one, then another, until you have used everything.

(4) Dot the top with the anchovies.

(5) Sprinkle the red wine vinegar, and oil from the artichokes and mushrooms over all.

(6) Cover with plastic wrap and let marinate for 1 hour.

(7) Garnish with parsley and basil leaves. Serve with frilly toothpicks.

NOTE: *All ingredients listed are easily available in your local markets.*

INGREDIENTS

9 3/4 ounces of olive condite
6 to 12 ounces of marinated artichoke hearts
6 ounces of colossal black olives
12 ounces of large stuffed green olives
6 ounces of pepperoncini
8 ounces of marinated mushrooms
7 ounces of pepperoni, cut into 1/4-inch circles
1/2 pound of provolone cheese, cut into 1/2 inch cubes
2 or 3 carrots, peeled and cut into sticks, 2-inches by a quarter inch
1 or 2 stalks celery, cut in half lengthwise, then into 2-inch sticks
2 medium tomatoes, stem end removed and cut into 6 wedges each
1 green and 1 red sweet pepper, seeded, and cut into strips
romaine leaves or other greens
2 ounces of oil packed, rolled anchovies with capers (add last)
red wine vinegar
oil from artichokes and mushrooms
parsley and small whole basil leaves

SERVES 8-10

YOGURT CHEESE
WITH ARUGULA AND LOVAGE

(1) Line a sieve with a coffee filter or a double layer of cheese cloth. Set the sieve over a bowl and pour in the yogurt. Cover the yogurt with plastic wrap.

(2) Refrigerate overnight for a minimum of 4 hours to let the yogurt liquid drain away. Discard the liquid and scrape the yogurt cheese into a bowl.

(3) Blend the herbs and onion into the yogurt. Grind pepper over all and mix. Taste and add a little salt, if desired.

(4) Serve with low-fat, whole grain crackers.

NOTE: *Be creative and add your own combination of herbs to the yogurt cheese.*

NOTE: *This is the perfect spread for those who wish to restrict fat, not flavor, in their diets.*

INGREDIENTS

8 ounces of non-fat, plain yogurt
1 tablespoon of finely minced arugula
1 tablespoon of finely minced tender young lovage leaves
2 or 3 green onions with part of the green tops, minced
A few grindings of fresh black pepper
salt to taste, if desired

SERVES 4

CARROT ORANGE SOUP

(1) In a 2-quart saucepan, heat oil and cook the onion, stirring, until softened.

(2) Add the carrots and boiling water. Bring the mixture to a boil, cover, and simmer for 15-20 minutes, or until carrots are tender.

(3) In a blender, purée the mixture until smooth. Transfer to a bowl, cool, and add the orange juice, rind, salt, and white pepper. Chill (see note).

(4) Whisk in the yogurt. The mixture should be smooth, creamy, and a beautiful orange color.

(5) Serve in chilled bowls garnished with lots of chopped chives.

NOTE: *To chill quickly, set the puréed mixture in a metal bowl over another bowl of ice before adding juice and yogurt.*

INGREDIENTS

2 tablespoons of vegetable oil
1/3 cup of onion, chopped
3 large carrots, peeled and thinly sliced
1 cup of boiling water
1/2 cup of fresh orange juice
1 teaspoon of grated orange rind
salt to taste (optional)
white pepper to taste
1/3 cup of plain, non-fat yogurt
freshly chopped chives

NOTE: *This is a low calorie, nutrient dense soup you can keep in the refrigerator to snack on without feeling guilty. It's a special first course for a summer dinner.*

SERVES 3-4

BASIC CHICKEN SOUP

(1) Wash the chicken parts well in cold water. Place in a 3-quart saucepan. Add water and bring to a boil. Reduce heat and simmer for a few minutes. Remove any froth as it appears and discard.

(2) Add the celery, carrot, onion, parsley, bay leaf, thyme, salt and pepper. Cover and simmer slowly for 45 minutes.

(3) Taste and add more salt and pepper as desired. If the flavor still needs lifting, add half a chicken bouillon cube. Taste again, and, if satisfactory, simmer another 15 minutes. Turn off heat.

(4) Cool and strain out the vegetables, herbs, and chicken parts. Pick pieces of chicken off bones and set aside. If using the soup as is, you can cut up the carrot pieces and put them back in the soup along with the chicken pieces.

NOTE: *There is usually enough chicken to make a salad for a sandwich.*

INGREDIENTS

1 1/2 pounds of chicken parts such as wing tips, necks, backs, thighs, legs, or half a 3-pound chicken
1 quart of water
1 stalk of celery plus the leafy tops from 2 stalks, cut in pieces
1 carrot, peeled and cut in chunks
1 medium onion, peeled and stuck with 3 whole cloves
2 sprigs of parsley with stems
1 bay leaf
2 sprigs of fresh thyme about 2 inches long or 1/4 teaspoon of dried thyme
1/4 teaspoon of white pepper
1/2 teaspoon of salt
chicken bouillon cube optional

NOTE: *This soup stands on its own or can be used as a base for other soups, for cooking rice, and for sauces. Soup is basically water enriched with meat, poultry, vegetable, and herb flavors.*

MAKES 1 QUART

CURRIED LENTIL SOUP

(1) In a deep saucepan or stock pot, heat the olive oil.
(2) Add the onion, carrots, and celery. Stir and sauté about 4 minutes.
(3) Add the garlic, ginger, pepper flakes, curry, coriander, cumin, oregano, cayenne pepper, and salt. Stir to combine and simmer for 5 minutes.
(4) Add the lentils. Stir to combine and simmer another 4 minutes.
(5) Add 6 cups of cold water. Cover and bring to a boil.
(6) Lower the heat and simmer, partially covered for about 45 minutes or until the lentils are tender.
(7) Cool and purée the soup in a food processor or blender until creamy.
(8) Transfer to a bowl, cover and refrigerate for at least one day. The soup will hold up to 4 days.
(9) If serving hot, reheat, add the amount of cream you prefer and heat through. If serving cold, stir cream into cold soup and serve.
(10) Garnish with a dollop of sour cream and a sprinkling of chopped scallions.

INGREDIENTS

6 tablespoons of olive oil
1 cup of diced onion
3/4 cup of diced carrots
1/2 cup of diced celery
2 cloves of garlic, minced
1 tablespoon of finely minced ginger
1/4 teaspoon of red pepper flakes(optional)
1/8 cup of curry powder
2 teaspoons crushed coriander seeds
1 tablespoon of crushed cumin seeds
1 tablespoon of minced oregano leaves
1/8 teaspoon of cayenne pepper
salt to taste
2 cups of lentils, rinsed
6 cups of water
1 to 1 1/2 cups of heavy cream or half and half
sour cream
chopped scallion

SERVES 6-8

CREAMY CORN SOUP WITH

GINGER AND LEMON GRASS

(1) Combine corn, chicken broth, lemon grass, and ginger in a 3-quart pan. Bring to a simmer over medium heat.

(2) Melt butter and sauté shallots in a small skillet. Add to corn mixture and simmer for 15 minutes.

(3) Purée soup, in batches, in food processor. Return mixture to pan and add milk or cream. Add salt and white pepper to taste. Simmer a few more minutes.

(4) Ladle soup into a cup. Sprinkle with your choice of garnish.

NOTE: *I mince lemon grass in a spice mill. If mincing by hand, crush first, then mince extremely fine as lemon grass is very fibrous. A 3-inch piece of a 1/2-inch thick lemon grass stalk should yield 1 tablespoon of minced lemon grass. Use the part closest to the root end. -JWM*

INGREDIENTS

3 cups of corn kernels, cooked
3 cups of chicken broth
1 tablespoon of minced fresh lemon grass (see note)
1 tablespoon of finely grated fresh ginger root
1 tablespoon of butter
1/4 cup of chopped shallots (2 large)
1/3 cup of low fat milk, light cream or evaporated skim milk
salt and white pepper to taste
fresh dillweed or cilantro, ground cumin or coriander seed

SERVES 4

FRESH TOMATO SOUP

(1) In a 2-quart saucepan heat the olive oil.
(2) Add the garlic and sauté until just firm, do not brown.
(3) Stir in the tomatoes and simmer for about 15 minutes until the color just starts to change from red to orange. Stir in the dill and the stock. Simmer for 20 minutes.
(4) Add salt and pepper to taste.
(5) Add the heavy cream to the soup, heat through.
(6) Add the nutmeg and sugar and reseason with salt and pepper.
(7) Serve in soup bowls with a garnish of sour cream and a sprig of dill.

NOTE: *Soup will hold in the refrigerator up to 3 days before the heavy cream is added.*

INGREDIENTS

2 tablespoons of virgin olive oil
2 small cloves of garlic, minced
4 cups of fresh tomatoes, peeled (see note), seeded, and chopped
1/4 cup of minced dill
3 cups of veal or chicken stock
salt
freshly ground pepper
1 cup of heavy cream or half and half
1 teaspoon of ground nutmeg
1 teaspoon of sugar
sour cream
sprigs of dill

NOTE: *To peel tomatoes, add them to boiling water. Boil for one minute or until skin starts to split. Remove with a slotted spoon and cool. Skin will peel right off.*

SERVES 4-6

GEORGE'S OYSTER STEW

(1) Sauté the bacon in a 2-quart saucepan until crisp. Using a slotted spoon, remove bacon and set aside for garnishing.
(2) Add the onion and celery to the drippings and sauté until soft, about 5 minutes. Using a slotted spoon, remove vegetables and set aside.
(3) Add the oysters to the pan adding a bit of extra butter if necessary to prevent sticking. Brown the oysters and transfer them to the dish with the onions and celery. Set the pan aside for later use.
(4) Pour 1/4 cup of milk into a medum saucepan, heat, and add the cornstarch and saffron. Simmer 1 minute, then add the rest of the milk and the cream. Stir and simmer just until thickened. Remove from heat.
(5) Return the 2-quart saucepan to the heat and pour in the Pernod. Simmer 1 minute.
(6) Add the oyster liquid and simmer 3 minutes.
(7) Add the milk mixture and heat through stirring constantly.
(8) Add the oysters and vegetables and stir in the butter one piece at a time until all is melted.
(9) Add lots of freshly ground pepper and salt to taste.
(10) Pour into soup dishes and garnish with bacon and sprigs of parsley and/or garlic chive heads.

NOTE: If you prefer a stew with more substance add 4 cooked, peeled, and diced potatoes.

NOTE: My husband became enthralled with the description of an oyster stew preparation in James Michener's book, "Chesapeake." Using his imagination he came up with this version hopefully as rich and creamy as the one Michener so aptly described. -MKP

INGREDIENTS

1/2 pound of bacon, diced
6 medium onions, diced
3 large stalks of celery, diced
3 dozen oysters, shucked, liquid reserved
4 cups of milk
2 level tablespoons of cornstarch
1/2 teaspoon of saffron threads or 1/4 teaspoon of powdered saffron
2 cups of heavy cream
1 tablespoon of Pernod (optional)
1 1/2 sticks of unsalted butter, cut into small pieces
lots of freshly ground pepper
salt to taste
8 sprigs of parsley or garlic chive heads

SERVES 8

GOLDEN SQUASH SOUP WITH SAVORY

(1) Remove the stem end and slice the young squash thinly.
(2) Melt the butter and sauté the shallots, just until translucent.
(3) Add squash slices and sauté another five minutes, using a stir-fry technique.
(4) Add broth, water, potatoes, carrot, savory, salt and pepper. Simmer for 20-30 minutes, or until all vegetables are tender.
(5) In batches, purée the vegetables in a food processor and return to the saucepan.
(6) Add evaporated skim milk. If soup is too thick, thin with some low-fat milk or more broth.
(7) Serve warm or chilled with snipped chives and a spoon of plain non-fat yogurt.

NOTE: *If you have a large 1 pound squash, peel it, cut it in quarters, remove the seeds, and slice each quarter into thin slices.*

INGREDIENTS

1 pound of small summer squash
3 tablespoons of butter
3 shallots, chopped
1 cup of beef or chicken broth
1 cup of water
3 medium potatoes, peeled, sliced thin
1 large carrot, peeled, sliced thin
2 teaspoons of minced winter savory
salt and freshly ground pepper to taste
1/2 cup of skim evaporated milk
low-fat milk or extra broth as needed
freshly snipped chives

NOTE: *Fresh thyme leaves can be used in place of savory.*

SERVES 4

CAJUN CRAB CAKES

(1) In a small saucepan, melt 2 tablespoons of butter, whisk in flour and add scalded milk all at once. Stir constantly for 2 minutes, until slightly thickened.
(2) Whisk in the mustard, buttermilk, or yolk.
(3) Stir in the red and green peppers and onion. Set aside.
(4) Combine the crabmeat, cilantro, oregano, garlic, jalapeno peppers, cayenne pepper, paprika, ground pepper, and salt.
(5) Gradually add the white sauce to the crabmeat; combine until the mixture clings together.
(6) Transfer to a bowl; chill for a few hours or overnight.
(7) Heat 2 tablespoons of butter and a 1/4 cup of oil in a large skillet.
(8) Shape the crabmeat mixture into eight 3-inch patties; coat with egg whites; then with crumbs. Fry until golden on both sides. Repeat with all the patties.
(9) Drain the patties on paper towels and serve with Cajun Mayonnaise.

INGREDIENTS

2 tablespoons of butter
2 tablespoons of flour
1/2 cup of milk, scalded
2 tablespoons of Dijon mustard
1/4 cup of buttermilk or 1 egg yolk
1/2 cup of minced red pepper
1/2 cup of minced green pepper
1/2 cup of minced onion
1 pound of lump crabmeat, picked over
1/4 cup of minced cilantro leaves
2 tablespoons of minced oregano leaves
2 cloves of garlic, minced
2 jalapeno peppers, cored, minced
1/4 teaspoon of cayenne pepper
1 teaspoon of paprika
freshly ground pepper
1 teaspoon of salt (optional)
4 tablespoons of butter
1/3 cup of vegetable oil
2 egg whites beaten with 2 tablespoons of water
1/2 cup of fine breadcrumbs
Cajun Mayonnaise (see page 59)

SERVES 4

BROILED SWORDFISH
WITH BASIL AND MUSTARD

Compound Butter

(1) In a bowl, blend butter, basil, mustard, lemon juice, and garlic.
(2) Tear off a 10-inch piece of wax or parchment paper. Scrape the butter mixture onto the center of the bottom quarter of the paper.
(3) Spread a bit of the butter along the opposite edge of the paper.
(4) Roll the paper around the butter, shaping it into a 1/4 pound (8 tablespoons) roll.
(5) Twist the ends of the paper and chill the roll in the refrigerator.

NOTE: *If you have the compound butter prepared ahead, and have the clarified butter on hand, the fish can be ready to serve in 10 minutes.*

(1) Brush each fish steak with clarified butter and sprinkle with the salt and pepper blend.
(2) Broil the fish approximately 3 minutes on each side, about 3 inches from the heat. Do not overcook. The rule of thumb is 10 minutes cooking time per inch, so thicker steaks cook longer than thin slices.
(3) When fish is done, place a dollop of the compound butter on top. As it melts, it becomes a delicious topping or sauce. Serve with lemon wedges.

NOTE: *To clarify butter, melt 1/2 stick slowly, then skim the clear layer off the top. Discard the milky solids that remain on the bottom of the pan. The clarified butter keeps well and will not burn as easily.*

INGREDIENTS

Compound Butter

1/4 pound of butter, softened
1/4 cup of chopped fresh basil
1 tablespoon of prepared mustard
2 tablespoons of freshly squeezed lemon juice
1/4 teaspoon of minced garlic

4 swordfish steaks, 6-8 ounces each
clarified butter (see note)
3 teaspoons of salt and 1 teaspoon of pepper, blended
compound butter (see above)

SERVES 4

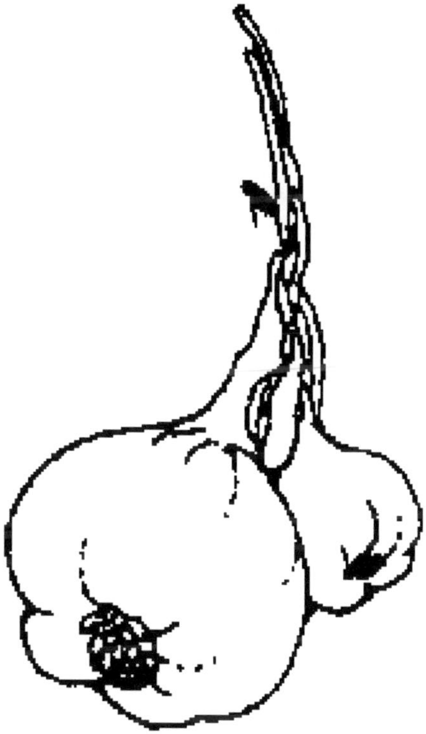

CURRIED SCALLOPS

(1) In a large sauté pan, melt the butter until bubbly.
(2) Add the scallions and sauté for 5 minutes or until limp.
(3) Add the garlic, oregano, tarragon, and curry. Sauté 2 minutes and then add the scallops in 3 batches, sautéing each batch until just firm, about 10 minutes. Transfer them to a dish to keep warm.
(4) Add the heavy cream or half and half to the pan. Simmer until slightly thickened, about 10 to 15 minutes.
(5) Just before serving, add the scallops and simmer for 3 more minutes coating them well with the sauce.
(6) Garnish with the extra scallion tops.

NOTE: *Serve with steamed rice and traditional curry garnishes; sliced bananas, peanuts, chutney, coconut, and raisins.*

INGREDIENTS

4 tablespoons of sweet butter
1 bunch scallions with tops, minced
1 large clove of garlic, minced
1 tablespoon of minced oregano leaves
1 teaspoon of minced tarragon leaves
1/4 cup of mild, medium or hot curry according to your taste
20 large sea scallops (5 per person)
1 1/2 cups of heavy cream or half and half
salt and pepper to taste
extra scallion tops, minced

SERVES 4

SALMON FILLETS
WITH GINGER, BASIL, AND TOMATOES

(1) Dust chopped tomatoes with sugar. Drain the tomatoes in a stainless steel colander for 20-25 minutes.
(2) Blot the tomatoes with paper towels to remove all excess moisture.
(3) Melt the butter in a medium-size skillet. Add the tomatoes; cook for 3 minutes over medium heat.
(4) Add salt, pepper, and cayenne pepper; set aside.
(5) Bring the fish stock to a simmer in a medium-size pan. Add the salmon fillet, cover, and turn off the heat. Steep for 30 minutes.
(6) While fish is steeping, combine the Tomato Concasse, sesame oil, and ginger; heat.
(7) When the tomato mixture is warm, add the basil and set aside.
(8) Carefully remove the fish from the cooking liquid with a large slotted spoon or a spatula onto a plate.
(9) Divide the fillet into 4 servings. Place on individual serving plates. Spoon ribbons of Tomato Concasse and Pesto over each serving.

INGREDIENTS

Tomato Concasse

1 1/2 to 2 pounds of fresh ripe tomatoes, peeled, seeded, and coarsely chopped (see page 19)
1 tablespoon of sugar
2 tablespoons of unsalted butter
salt and freshly ground pepper to taste
dash of cayenne pepper

16 ounces of homemade fish stock or bottled clam juice
1 to 1 1/4 pounds of salmon fillet, skinned
1 cup of Tomato Concasse (see above)
2 tablespoons of sesame oil
1 teaspoon of finely chopped fresh ginger
1 tablespoon of chopped fresh basil
1/4 cup of Pesto without the cheese (see page 43)

SERVES 4

FRESH TUNA
WITH ROSEMARY AND THYME

(1) Prepare the tuna by marinating it for 2 hours in a mixture of the white wine, 1 tablespoon of rosemary, and 1/2 tablespoon of thyme.

(2) Whisk together 1/2 cup of the olive oil, vinegar, and the remaining rosemary and thyme. Season with salt and pepper to taste and toss with the potatoes. Set aside.

(3) When ready to cook remove the tuna from the marinade, brush with the remaining olive oil and sprinkle some salt and pepper on both sides. Discard the marinade.

(4) Heat a regular skillet, a gridded pan or an outdoor grill to very hot.

(5) Grill the tuna for 5 minutes on each side for rare, 8 to 10 minutes for medium and 10 to 12 minutes for well done.

(6) Transfer to a platter to cool slightly.

(7) Divide the greens among four dinner plates and place a tuna steak in the center of each. Add some of the potatoes to each plate and top with any remaining dressing from the potatoes.

NOTE: *The subtle taste of tuna is enhanced but not overwhelmed by the pungent flavor of the rosemary. The tuna can be served as a steak for a dinner course or sliced when cool and served in a salad or as an appetizer. Tuna slices best when it is rare or medium and it should be sliced against the grain.*

INGREDIENTS

4 1-inch thick tuna steaks
1 cup of white wine
2 tablespoons of rosemary needles
1 tablespoon of thyme leaves
3/4 cup of olive oil
2 tablespoons of white vinegar
salt to taste
freshly ground pepper to taste
4 medium potatoes, boiled, peeled, and diced
4 cups of assorted greens, rinsed, and broken into small pieces, i.e., romaine, Boston or red leaf lettuce, radicchio, or arugula

SERVES 4

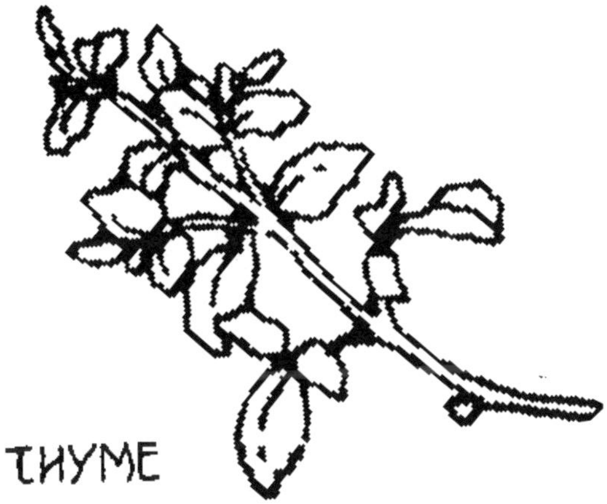

SHRIMP WITH OREGANO

Preheat oven to 350° F.

(1) Wash shrimp and drain well on paper towels.
(2) Arrange shrimp in a single layer in a 9-inch glass pie plate. Sprinkle with the lemon juice.
(3) In a small skillet, heat olive oil and butter until bubbly. Add crumbs, garlic, parsley, oregano, and pepper flakes. Stir and cook until crumbs are starting to brown. Remove from heat, add cheese and blend.
(4) Spoon crumb mixture over shrimp.
(5) Bake for 15 minutes. If crumbs aren't browned, broil 5 inches from heat, for about 3 minutes.
(6) Serve immediately, garnished with lemon wedges and oregano sprigs.

NOTE: *To serve as a first course, bake in 6 large scallop shells.*

INGREDIENTS

1 pound of medium shrimp, shelled and deveined
2 tablespoons of fresh lemon juice
3 tablespoons of olive oil
2 tablespoons of butter
3/4 cup of herb seasoned stuffing, whirred in a food processor to make 1/2 cup of fine crumbs
2 cloves of garlic, peeled and minced
2 tablespoons of chopped fresh parsley
1 tablespoon of fresh golden oregano or regular oregano
1/4 teaspoon of hot pepper flakes
2 tablespoons of grated Parmesan or Romano cheese
lemon wedges
oregano sprigs

SERVES 4

THYME CRUSTED PORK CHOPS

Preheat oven to 350° F.

(1) Prepare a baking pan by lining with aluminum foil and adding a rack for baking.
(2) In a bowl wide enough to hold a chop, combine the crumbs, thyme, salt and pepper. Pour the milk into a similar bowl.
(3) Coat the chops with the milk, then heavily coat with the crumbs.
(4) Lay the chops on the rack and bake in a pre-heated oven for about 1 1/2 hours turning once until they are crisp on both sides.
(5) While the chops are baking melt the butter in a sauté pan until bubbly. Add the apple slices and sauté on both sides until slightly browned.
(6) Serve chops with a few overlapping slices of the apples, garnishing each with a sprig of thyme or parsley.

INGREDIENTS

2 cups of fine bread crumbs
1/3 cup of fresh thyme leaves
1 teaspoon of salt
1 teaspoon of ground pepper
2 cups of milk
4 large or 8 small pork chops, 1-inch thick
4 tablespoons of sweet butter
3 Granny Smith apples, peeled, cored and cut into 1/2-inch circles
4 sprigs of thyme or parsley

NOTE: This recipe is particularly good in the winter. Serve the chops with either mashed potatoes, potato pancakes, or corn fritters.

SERVES 4

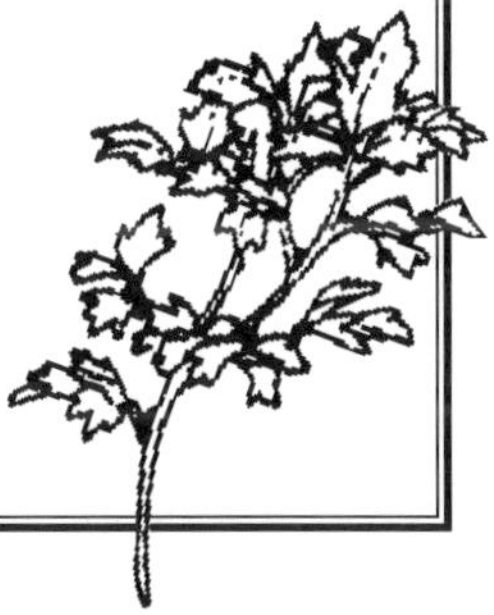

PORK FILET
WITH APRICOTS AND PRUNES

Preheat oven to 350° F.

(1) Place the apricots and prunes in a bowl and add the wine. Marinate in the refrigerator overnight.
(2) The next day, brush the filet of pork with olive oil and sprinkle with salt and pepper.
(3) In a small bowl combine the tarragon and savory and with your fingers pat onto the pork to coat.
(4) Place the filet on the rack of a roasting pan. Add l-inch of water to the pan, the bouquet garni, and the chopped onion.
(5) For the first hour of roasting add enough water to maintain a l-inch level.
(6) Continue to roast for 1 1/2 to 2 hours or 30 minutes to a pound, allowing onions to darken but not burn. Add a bit of extra water if the onions get too dark.
(7) When the roast is done transfer to a platter to keep warm. Remove the rack and place the pan over medium heat and skim off any fat.
(8) Add the apricots, prunes, small onions, and l cup of the marinade. Scrape down the sides of the pan with a spatula. Simmer about 7 minutes.
(9) Remove the bouquet garni and discard. Whisk in the butter mixture in small chunks. As it simmers, the sauce will thicken slightly.

(10) Add the sugar and reseason with salt and pepper to your taste. Transfer to a saucepan and keep warm until ready to serve.

(11) Slice the pork and serve with a dollop of the sauce and two each of the apricots, prunes, and onions.

NOTE: Accompany with Savory Rice (see page 38) or Crispy Potatoes with Herbs (see page 51), turnips, or squash. This is a perfect example of comfort food - food that satisfies the stomach and the mind. It is particularly satisfying in the fall and winter.

INGREDIENTS

8 dried apricots
8 dried prunes
3 cups of red wine
1 pork filet, rolled and tied, about 3 to 5 pounds
1/4 cup of olive oil
salt and pepper to your taste
3 tablespoons of minced tarragon
3 tablespoons of minced winter savory
Bouquet Garni (see Herbal Hint #19, page 5)
1 large onion, coarsely chopped
12 small onions, boil 5 minutes and peel
3 tablespoons of butter kneaded with 1 tablespoon of flour
1 teaspoon of sugar
salt and pepper

SERVES 4

ROAST LEG OF LAMB
WITH GARLIC AND OREGANO

Preheat oven to 325° F.

(1) Remove lamb from refrigerator 1/2 hour before roasting.
(2) Wipe lamb with a clean, damp cloth. Trim off any excess fat.
(3) With a small, sharp, pointed knife, make a slit in the lamb 1/2 to 1-inch deep. Slip a slice of garlic into the slit. Continue to make slits and insert garlic all around the roast, 10-12 times.
(4) Rub the roast all over with olive oil.
(5) Sprinkle with salt and pepper and the dried oregano.
(6) Squeeze lemon juice over all.
(7) Lay the celery stalks in a suitable size roasting pan. Place the lamb on top with the fat side up.
(8) Roast, allowing about 16 minutes per pound for medium rare, about 21 minutes for well done.
(9) When the roast is done remove it from the oven and let stand about 10 minutes before carving.
(10) Serve with mint sauce, (see page 47), or mint jelly. Garnish with fresh mint leaves.

NOTE: Serve with Crispy Potatoes with Herbs (see page 51).

SERVES 4-6

INGREDIENTS

3 to 4 pounds of shank half leg of lamb
3 cloves of garlic, peeled and thinly sliced
2 tablespoons of olive oil
salt and freshly ground black pepper
1 teaspoon of dried oregano
1 lemon, cut in half, seeds removed
4 stalks of celery, trimmed

SOUTHWESTERN PICADILLO

INGREDIENTS

2 tablespoons of vegetable oil
1 medium onion, chopped
1 1/2 pounds of lean ground beef
16 ounces of whole tomatoes, undrained, coarsely chopped
6 ounces of tomato paste
1/2 cup of raisins
2 tablespoons of red wine vinegar or sherry vinegar
2 tablespoons of Chili Powder or to taste (see Herbal Hint #22, page 5)
1 teaspoon of ground cinnamon
1 teaspoon of ground cumin
pinch of ground cloves
1 teaspoon of sugar
2 cups of sliced fresh mushrooms
1/2 cup of toasted chopped almonds
2 or 3 jalapeno peppers, seeded, and finely diced

SERVES 6-8

(1) Heat the oil in a large skillet over medium heat.
(2) Add the onion and sauté until translucent.
(3) Increase heat and add the beef. Brown lightly.
(4) Add the tomatoes, tomato paste, raisins, vinegar, spices, and sugar to the skillet.
(5) Cover the pan and simmer for about 1 hour. Stir in the mushrooms, almonds, and jalapenos. Simmer another 30 minutes. Serve with rice, or fill tacos with the mixture, or bake in little turnovers called empanadas.

NOTE: *Flavors of the American Southwest are pungent, with ground chili peppers used in abundance. Don't be intimidated, however. This dish is mellowed with other ingredients that cut the heat of the jalapenos.*

CHICKEN WITH
BLACK OLIVES AND THYME

Preheat oven to 350° F.

(1) Place the chicken in a large baking dish.
(2) Add the onions, garlic, oregano, thyme, olives, potatoes, wine, and a sprinkling of salt and pepper.
(3) Bake for 45 minutes, turning the chicken and potatoes a few times.
(4) Add the mushrooms, and combine with the chicken.
(5) Bake until the chicken is tender and the skin is crisp.
(6) Remove from the oven and let sit about 10 minutes.
(7) Transfer to a serving platter. Nap with natural pan sauce and garnish with fresh oregano and thyme.

NOTE: *This is the perfect one dish meal for family and friends.*

INGREDIENTS

3 1/2 to 4-pound chicken cut into serving pieces plus 1 chicken breast, cut into four pieces
2 large onions, sliced
1 large clove of garlic, minced
2 tablespoons of fresh minced oregano leaves
1 tablespoon of fresh whole thyme leaves
2 cups of pitted black sweet olives, halved
4 medium potatoes, quartered
1 cup of white wine
salt and pepper to taste
3/4 pound of mushrooms, sliced
sprigs of fresh thyme and oregano

SERVES 4-6

ROAST CHICKEN WITH PESTO

Preheat oven to 350° F.

(1) Wash chicken inside and out and pat dry.
(2) Salt the cavity and the skin, rubbing it in as much as possible.
(3) Use a wooden spoon handle and carefully insert it under the breast skin. Loosen the skin from the breast flesh, then work the handle into the thigh and leg areas as far as you can
(4) Use a teaspoon to insert the pesto between the skin and the flesh. Push a spoonful in as far as you can and spread it around. Coat all the loosened areas.
(5) Tie the legs and wings so they stay close to the chicken's body.
(6) Brush chicken with melted butter and roast for 30 minutes. Baste with pan drippings. Roast another 30 minutes or until skin is crisp and brown and thigh juices run clear.

INGREDIENTS

3 to4 pound whole chicken
1/2 cup of Pesto Sauce, (see page 43), made without the cheese
salt
2 tablespoons of butter, melted

---

(7) Remove from oven and let stand for 10 minutes before carving.
(8) Serve with pasta or rice and a salad.

NOTE *If desired, you can spread pesto under the skin of cut up pieces and broil or bake them. This chicken is also delicious at room temperature, served at a buffet or picnic.*

SERVES 4

CORNISH GAME HENS
WITH SAVORY RICE

Preheat oven to 350° F.

(1) Pour 1-inch of water into roasting pan large enough to hold the four hens. Place a roasting rack into the pan.
(2) Rinse the hens, tuck in the wing tips to secure, and with your fingers make a separation between the breast skin and flesh and insert a sprig of tarragon on each side.
(3) Place 1 piece of apple into the cavity of each hen and coat hens with the olive oil.
(4) Combine the garlic, 1 tablespoon of tarragon, 1 tablespoon of marjoram, and black pepper, and sprinkle over the top of the hens.
(5) Add the onions to the pan water and place the hens on the rack.
(6) Bake for 45 minutes or until all the water evaporates and the onions are well browned but not burned. Add the white wine, 1/2 cup of water, and mushrooms.
(7) Bake another 30 minutes or until hens are golden and the juices run clear when the hens are pierced with a fork.
(8) While the hens are roasting, reheat the rice and combine with the butter, remaining tarragon, parsley, marjoram, and salt and pepper to taste. Set aside, covered to keep warm.
(9) When the hens are done transfer to a serving platter. Remove the rack and place the pan over a medium heat to finish the sauce.

(10) Add some water to the pan and scrape down the sides. Simmer 5 minutes and transfer to a smaller pan to keep warm.

(11) To serve, place each hen on a dinner plate and mound some of the rice around the hens spooning some into the opening. Dollop on some of the sauce. Serve with Green Beans Hemingway (see page 54), a salad, and crusty bread.

NOTE: *The pan drippings will make a small amount of natural sauce to nap onto the hens.*

INGREDIENTS

4 Cornish game hens
8 sprigs of tarragon
1 apple, quartered
1/2 cup of olive oil
2 cloves of garlic, minced
1 tablespoon of minced tarragon
1 tablespoon of minced marjoram
1 teaspoon of black pepper
1 large onion, diced
1 cup of white wine
1/2 cup of water
1/2 pound of mushrooms, quartered
3 cups of cooked white rice
6 tablespoons of butter
1 tablespoon of minced tarragon
1 tablespoon of minced flat leaf parsley
1 tablespoon of minced marjoram
salt and pepper to taste

SERVES 4

STUFFED CHICKEN BREAST
WITH BASIL

(1) Butterfly each breast half down the center vertically to form a heart shaped cutlet. Do not cut through the center.
(2) Pound the cutlets between 2 pieces of waxed paper with a heavy bottomed glass or meat pounder to form a thin cutlet. Set aside. Your butcher can do this for you.
(3) For the filling, blend the cheese, walnuts, and butter in a medium bowl. Add pepper and thyme.
(4) Brush each of the cutlets with a bit of olive oil on the open side and place a basil or spinach leaf on one half. Spread some of the cheese mix on top of the leaf and cover with a second leaf.
(5) Fold the unstuffed half over to form a package and brush all sides with olive oil.
(6) Heat a large skillet or an outdoor grill. (Lightly oil skillet.)
(7) Grill the breasts about 7 minutes on each side until chicken is firm to the touch.
(8) Transfer to a plate and allow to cool slightly.
(9) Serve with Savory Rice (see page 38). Garnish with fresh thyme and basil.

INGREDIENTS

2 large chicken breasts, boned and halved
3 ounces of chevre (goat cheese) or cream cheese, softened
1/2 cup of walnuts, finely chopped
2 tablespoons of sweet butter, softened
coarsely ground pepper
2 tablespoons of thyme leaves
1/3 cup of olive oil
8 large basil leaves or 8 pieces of steamed spinach leaves
fresh thyme and basil sprigs

NOTE: This dish is excellent for an outdoor party.

SERVES 4

PARSLIED TURKEY CUTLETS

(1) Combine the first 8 ingredients in a medium bowl. Add the cutlets. Marinate for 3 to 4 hours or overnight in the refrigerator.
(2) In a food processor or a blender, process the parsley, basil, spinach, and garlic for 7 to 10 seconds.
(3) Add the crumbs, salt, and black pepper. Process 5 seconds.
(4) Keep the machine running and add the olive oil in a steady stream. Stop once to scrape down the sides.
(5) Add the Madeira and process 3 seconds.
(6) Transfer to a bowl, cover, and refrigerate 3 to 4 hours or overnight.
(7) Heat the oil and butter in a skillet or heat an outdoor grill.
(8) With a spatula, spread parsley mixture onto both sides of the cutlets; sauté or grill 5 minutes on each side.
(9) Transfer to a serving platter. Serve with Garlic Roasted Beets (see page 53) and steamed rice.

INGREDIENTS

1 tablespoon of minced sage leaves
1 tablespoon of thyme leaves
1/3 cup of minced flat leaf parsley
1 clove of garlic, minced
1 teaspoon of black pepper
1/2 cup of medium dry Madeira
1/2 teaspoon of salt
1/4 cup of olive oil
1 3/4 to 2 pounds of turkey cutlets
1/2 cup of tightly packed flat leaf parsley
1/3 cup of tightly packed basil leaves
1/3 cup of tightly packed spinach leaves
1 large clove of garlic, cut in half
1/4 cup of fine bread crumbs
1 1/2 teaspoons of salt
1 1/2 teaspoons of black pepper
1/4 cup of olive oil
1/4 cup of medium dry Madeira
1/4 to 1/3 cup of peanut oil
4 tablespoons of butter

SERVES 4

TURKEY SAUSAGE

(1) Heat the oil in a skillet over medium heat. Add garlic and onion and sauté for five minutes, stirring constantly. Onions should be just translucent. Allow to cool for five minutes.
(2) Combine the onion mixture with the turkey, pepper flakes, cayenne, salt, sage, bread crumbs, fennel seeds, and cider vinegar.
(3) Form into six patties.
(4) Lightly oil a skillet and brown patties over medium heat until cooked through but still moist inside (about 8 minutes).
(5) Serve immediately.

NOTE: *If you mix uncooked onion and garlic into sausage or meatloaf and let the mixture stand, the onion and garlic flavors become too strong. This recipe makes delicious patties, much lower in fat than traditional pork sausage. Game turkey are native to the Americas, as are all sweet and hot peppers.*

INGREDIENTS

1 tablespoon of vegetable oil
1 small clove of garlic, minced
1/2 cup of finely chopped onion
1 pound of ground turkey
1/2 to 1 teaspoon of red pepper flakes (depending on your taste)
1/4 teaspoon of cayenne pepper
1/4 teaspoon of salt
1 teaspoon of finely minced fresh sage
1/2 cup of plain bread crumbs
1 tablespoon of fennel seeds, whirred in a spice mill or crushed
1 tablespoon of cider vinegar
oil for sautéing

SERVES 4

BASIL (PESTO) SAUCE

(1) In a small skillet, lightly toast the walnuts and pignoli nuts.
(2) In a processor or blender, process the basil, nuts, garlic, salt, and 1/2 cup of olive oil for about 30 seconds.
(3) With the machine running, add the remaining oil through the feed tube and process until well blended.
(4) Add the cheeses and black pepper and process a few seconds.
(5) Serve the pesto with penne shaped pasta, or wherever pesto sauce is needed in a recipe.

NOTE: *To serve 4, cook 3/4 of a pound of pasta in a generous amount of boiling salted water. While pasta is cooking, take 2 or 3 tablespoons of the boiling water and add to 3/4 cup of the sauce before tossing it with the pasta. Serve with extra Parmesan and freshly ground black pepper.*

INGREDIENTS

2 tablespoons of walnut pieces
6 tablespoons of pignoli nuts
3 cups of tightly packed basil, leaves
3 cloves of garlic, minced
1/2 teaspoon of coarse salt
1 1/4 cup of extra virgin olive oil, divided
3/4 cup of grated Romano cheese
1/4 cup of grated Parmesan cheese (best quality you can buy)
freshly ground black pepper

MAKES 3 CUPS

BASIC TOMATO SAUCE

(1) Heat olive oil in large skillet, over medium heat.
(2) Add garlic and onion and sauté until golden. *DO NOT BROWN.*
(3) Coarsely chop the whole tomatoes just enough to break them up.
(4) Add the tomato paste to the sautéed onions. Stir to blend.
(5) Add the coarsely chopped tomatoes, bay leaf, oregano, basil, parsley, sugar, red pepper flakes, salt and pepper.
(6) Add some water if sauce seems too thick. Cover and simmer for 20 minutes, then adjust seasonings to your taste.
(7) Let simmer, covered, on lowest heat setting, for about 1 hour.
(8) You may add meatballs.

NOTE: The secret to tender meatballs is to use stale Italian bread that has been soaked in cold water and squeezed out, rather than bread crumbs. Sauté meatballs separately and add to the sauce to simmer.

INGREDIENTS

3 tablespoons of olive oil
1 or 2 cloves of garlic, minced or put through a garlic press
1 medium onion, chopped or grated
28 ounces of whole tomatoes in purée
6 ounces of tomato paste
1 bay leaf
2 teaspoons of chopped oregano
1 tablespoon of torn basil leaves
1 tablespoon of chopped flat leaf parsley
1/2 teaspoon of sugar
a good pinch of red pepper flakes
salt and pepper to taste
water, as needed

MAKES 1 to 1 1/2 QUARTS

CURRIED APPLE CHUTNEY

(1) In a stainless steel saucepan, heat the apples, onion, white sugar, and raisins. Cover and simmer 15 minutes over a medium heat. Stir from time to time. Cook until apples start to melt down and form a sauce. Add a bit of water if the apples are not juicy and start to stick.
(2) Mash the apples but leave some chunks for texture.
(3) Add the brown sugar, mustard seed, dill, Worcestershire sauce, vinegar, cinnamon, and curry powder. Combine well and simmer partially covered for 20 minutes, stirring frequently.
(4) Cool and store in a glass, ceramic, or stainless steel container.
(5) Serve to accompany potato pancakes, roasts, or poultry.

NOTE: This will keep for a month or more in the refrigerator and tends to become more flavorful as time passes.

INGREDIENTS

6 Granny Smith or golden delicious apples, peeled, cored, and cut into chunks
1 medium onion, minced
3/4 cup of white sugar
1/2 cup of golden raisins
1/4 cup of brown sugar
1 teaspoon of mustard seed, crushed
1 teaspoon of minced dill
1 tablespoon of Worcestershire sauce
2 tablespoons of balsamic vinegar
1/2 teaspoon of cinnamon
2 tablespoons of curry powder

MAKES 2 CUPS

GINGERY CRANBERRY RELISH

(1) Mix together the cranberries, onion, sweet peppers, sugar, ginger root, and lemon grass in a glass bowl.
(2) Heat oil in a non-stick pan, add cranberry mixture and heat to bubbling. Cook one minute.
(3) Add lime juice, jalapeno, and tomato. Remove from heat.
(4) Add the cumin and stir.
(5) Serve warm or at room temperature. Drain off excess liquid, if desired.

NOTE: *Good served with chicken, turkey, or pork. Try it with the Turkey Sausage (see page 42). This recipe combines American cranberries with Pacific Rim flavors plus a touch of the Southwest.*

INGREDIENTS

1 cup of fresh or frozen cranberries, coarsely chopped
1/4 cup of chopped red onion
1/4 cup of chopped sweet green pepper
1/4 cup of chopped yellow or red pepper
1/4 cup of sugar
1 1/2 teaspoons of freshly grated ginger root
1 1/2 teaspoons of finely minced lemon grass (bulb part only)
1 tablespoon of safflower oil
1 tablespoon of fresh lime juice
1/2 jalapeno pepper, finely diced
1 small tomato, peeled, seeded, and diced small
1/2 teaspoon of ground cumin

MAKES 2 CUPS

MINT MARINATED CARROTS

INGREDIENTS

4 large carrots, peeled and sliced thin
1/2 teaspoon of salt for cooking water
2 tablespoons of cider vinegar
6 tablespoons of water, divided
1/4 cup of mint leaves, chopped
2 tablespoons of fresh lemon juice
2 1/2 teaspoons of sugar
1/4 teaspoon of salt

(1) Cook the carrot slices in a very small amount of salted water, covered, over low heat for 10 minutes or until carrots are crisp and tender. Set aside.
(2) Bring the vinegar and half of the water to a boil.
(3) Pour over half the mint leaves. Let stand 15 minutes.
(4) Strain the mint leaves from the vinegar mixture. Add the remaining 3 tablespoons of water, lemon juice, sugar, and salt. Chill. Add remaining mint leaves.
(5) Drain carrots, place in a glass bowl, and pour enough mint sauce over them to cover.
(6) Marinate for at least 1 hour or overnight in refrigerator.

NOTE: *You may also use the mint sauce to marinate string beans or serve it with roast lamb or lamb chops.*

SERVES 4

ZUCCHINI PICKLES

(1) Thinly slice the zucchini.
(2) Quarter the onions and slice them thin.
(3) Place the zucchini and onions in a glass bowl and add enough water to cover the vegetables. Add the salt. Let stand for 2 hours. Drain thoroughly.
(4) Bring vinegar, sugar, celery seed, turmeric, and mustard seed to a boil and pour over vegetables. Let stand for 2 hours.
(5) Transfer the vegetable mixture to a 2-quart pan and bring to a boil. Boil for 5 minutes.
(6) Pack in hot sterilized jars and seal.

NOTE: *If you've never made pickles, these are perfect for a first timer.*

INGREDIENTS

2 pounds of zucchini, small to medium size, unpeeled
2 small onions, peeled
1/4 cup of Kosher (coarse) salt
2 cups of white vinegar
2 cups of sugar
1 teaspoon of celery seed
1 teaspoon of turmeric
2 teaspoons of mustard seed

MAKES 3 PINTS

RED PEPPER RELISH

(1) Finely dice the peppers and onions and combine in a bowl.
(2) Add the dill. Pour boiling water over all and allow to steep for 15 minutes.
(3) Drain and transfer peppers and onions to a saucepan. Add the vinegar, sugar, salt, and jalapeno. Bring to a boil and simmer over a medium heat for 20 minutes.
(4) Spoon into glass, ceramic, or stainless steel containers. Cool, cover, and keep in the refrigerator. This will hold for a few weeks.
(5) Serve as a condiment with sandwiches or roasts.

NOTE: *Add the jalapeno pepper seeds for extra spiciness.*

INGREDIENTS

6 red peppers, cored
3 medium onions, peeled
1/4 cup of minced dill
4 cups of boiling water
1/2 cup of vinegar
1/2 cup of sugar
1/2 teaspoon of salt
1 jalapeno pepper, minced

MAKES ABOUT 3 CUPS

BRAISED FENNEL
WITH BARLEY

(1) Heat butter and oil in a large skillet. Sauté onion until translucent.
(2) Add the chopped fennel, stir and sauté for 2 minutes.
(3) Add the barley, stir, and sauté another minute.
(4) Add 1/4 cup of heated broth and the wine. Let it bubble up and add another 1/4 cup of broth.
(5) Add the tomato, basil, pepper flakes, salt and pepper.
(6) Add another 1/2 cup of broth, turn heat to low, cover, and let simmer about 10 minutes. Check and add more broth, as needed.
(7) Simmer for 30 to 40 minutes or until the barley is tender and liquid is absorbed, adding extra liquid if necessary.
(8) Serve garnished with basil and parsley.

NOTE: *This recipe can be a vegetarian entrée by substituting hot vegetable broth for the chicken broth.*

INGREDIENTS

1 tablespoon of butter
1 tablespoon of olive oil
1 medium onion, chopped
1 fennel bulb, about 10 ounces, trimmed and finely chopped
1/2 cup of barley, medium or fine grain
1 to 1 1/2 cups of hot chicken broth (see page 16)
1/4 cup of dry white wine
1 medium tomato, peeled, seeded, and diced
2 tablespoons of fresh basil, chopped
1/4 teaspoon of hot pepper flakes
salt and freshly ground black pepper, to taste
basil and parsley, chopped

SERVES 4-6

CRISPY POTATOES
WITH HERBS

Preheat oven to 350° F.

(1) Place the potatoes in a baking pan and add the olive oil to coat.
(2) Sprinkle on the thyme, oregano, rosemary, bay leaf, lemon sage, garlic, peppers, and salt to your taste.
(3) Bake for 45 minutes, shaking the pan a few times, or until the potatoes are crisp and tender.
(4) Discard the bay leaf and serve with meat, chicken, or seafood.

NOTE: *These make an excellant accompaniment to Roast Leg of Lamb (see page 34).*

INGREDIENTS

8 large Russet or Bliss potatoes, skin on, rinsed, and cut into quarters
1/3 cup of olive oil
1 tablespoon of thyme leaves
1 tablespoon of minced oregano leaves
1 tablespoon of rosemary needles, crushed
1 large bay leaf
1 tablespoon of minced lemon sage leaves
2 cloves of garlic, peeled and sliced
freshly ground pepper
cayenne pepper
salt to taste

SERVES 4-6

SOUTHWESTERN EGGPLANT
CASSEROLE

Preheat oven to 350° F.

(1) Salt each slice of eggplant and form 3 or 4 stacks on a plate. Cover with another plate to weight down the slices; let stand 30 minutes. Pour off liquid as it accumulates. Pat dry.

(2) Sauté bacon over medium heat until not quite crisp. Drain off all but two tablespoons of the accumulated fat.

(3) Add the onion and red pepper. Sauté for one minute.

(4) Add tomatoes, jalapeno, chili powder, cumin, sugar, salt and pepper to taste. Simmer for 20 minutes.

(5) Flour eacheggplant slice, brush with olive oil. Bake in a single layer on a baking sheet for 15 minutes, turning once.

(6) Oil a 2-quart casserole. Arrange a layer of eggplant slices on bottom. Nap with some sauce, repeat, ending with sauce.

(7) Top with the grated cheese.

(8) Bake for 30 to 40 minutes, or until cheese is lightly browned.

INGREDIENTS

1 large eggplant, 1 1/4 to 1 1/2 pounds, peeled and sliced into 1/2-inch thick slices
2 slices of bacon, chopped
1 large onion, chopped
1 sweet red pepper, seeded, and diced
1 pound, 12 ounces of tomatoes, drained, and slightly crushed
1 small jalapeno pepper, seeded, and finely diced
1 teaspoon of Chili Powder (see Herbal Hint #22, page 5)
1/2 teaspoon of ground cumin
1/2 teaspoon of sugar
salt and pepper to taste
flour for dredging
olive oil
1 cup of grated Monterey Jack cheese

SERVES 4-6

GARLIC ROASTED BEETS

Preheat oven to 350° F.

(1) Rinse beets, and cut a small piece from the top and bottom.
(2) Cut the beets in half and place in a baking pan. Add 1/4 cup of olive oil and turn the beets to coat with oil.
(3) Sprinkle on the garlic, oregano, tarragon, thyme, pepper and salt. Turn beets to coat with the herbs.
(4) Bake for 50 minutes or until a fork easily pierces them. Shake the pan a few times while cooking.
(5) When cooked remove from the oven, cover to keep warm.
(6) While the beets are roasting rinse the tops well and coarsely chop.
(7) Heat remaining olive oil in a sauté pan; add the tops. Sauté, stirring frequently, until the tops are wilted and all the liquid has evaporated.
(8) Add some salt and pepper to taste.
(9) Cut each beet half into 4 pieces, and toss with the pan drippings.
(10) To serve, portion out the tops and add the diced beets on top, covering with the pan juices.

INGREDIENTS

12 medium to large unpeeled beets with tops removed
1/2 cup of virgin olive oil
3 cloves of garlic, minced
1 tablespoon of minced oregano leaves
1 tablespoon of minced tarragon
1 tablespoon of thyme leaves
1 teaspoon of ground black pepper
salt to taste

NOTE: When beets are prepared in this manner they take on an entirely new character. This recipe goes well with meat roasts, poultry, and fish.

SERVES 4-6

GREEN BEANS HEMINGWAY

❧ INGREDIENTS

2 tablespoons of olive oil
1 large clove of garlic, minced
1 tablespoon of fresh chopped oregano leaves
1 tablespoon of fresh rosemary needles, chopped
1 tablespoon of minced fresh parsley leaves
1 tablespoon of pepper
1 teaspoon of salt
2 large ripe tomatoes, diced
4 cups of cooked green beans cut into 3-inch pieces

(1) Heat oil in a medium skillet.
(2) Add the garlic, oregano, rosemary, parsley, pepper and salt.
(3) Sauté for 3 minutes, do not allow the garlic to burn.
(4) Gradually, in two additions, add the tomatoes and cook over high heat for a total of 7 minutes, stirring frequently. The diced tomato should remain quite firm with a fresh tomato aroma.
(5) Add the beans and combine to warm through.
(6) Serve warm with poultry, meat, or fish.

NOTE: *Inspired by an Ernest Hemingway story, this recipe captures the flavor of the 1930's.*

SERVES 4

PEPPERS WITH SAGE

(1) Heat the olive oil in a large skillet.
(2) Add the garlic, sage, oregano, salt and pepper. Sauté 3 minutes.
(3) Add the peppers, sauté 5 minutes, stirring frequently.
(4) Add the onion, sauté 5 minutes or until limp. Peppers will remain fairly firm.
(5) Transfer to a serving dish and garnish with sprigs of sage.

NOTE: *Serve warm as a side dish with roasts or fish or serve at room temperature as a salad or appetizer.*

INGREDIENTS

1/3 cup of olive oil
1 clove of garlic, minced
2 tablespoons of minced sage leaves
1 tablespoon of minced oregano leaves
1 teaspoon of salt
1 1/2 teaspoons of ground pepper
2 medium red peppers, cored and sliced into thin slivers
1 medium green pepper, cored and sliced into thin slivers
1 medium yellow pepper, cored and sliced into thin slivers
1 large red onion, peeled and sliced into thin circles
sprigs of sage

SERVES 4

STUFFED MUSHROOMS

Preheat oven to 375° F.

(1) Remove stems from mushrooms, trimming bottom of stems as necessary.
(2) Chop the stems into fairly small pieces.
(3) Pour a tablespoon or two of the olive oil into a medium sized skillet and lightly sauté the mushroom stems.
(4) Add the remaining olive oil, bread crumbs, torn basil, oregano, parsley, tomatoes, and cheese. Mix gently and remove from heat.
(5) Use the oil from the tomatoes to grease the bottom of a casserole that will hold the 12 mushroom caps. Set the caps in the dish.
(6) Fill the caps with the bread crumb mixture and bake for 10 minutes or until crumb mixture is crisp and brown.

NOTE: *These can be used as a side dish or an hors d'oeuvre.*

INGREDIENTS

12 large white mushrooms, wiped clean with a damp paper towel
1/3 cup of olive oil, divided
1/2 cup of unseasoned bread crumbs
1 tablespoon of torn basil leaves
1/2 teaspoon of dried oregano
2 tablespoons of minced flat leaf parsley
2 tablespoons of finely minced sun dried tomatoes in oil
1/2 cup of grated Parmesan cheese
1 tablespoon of oil from the sun dried tomatoes

SERVES 4-6

TOMATOES, BASIL,
AND RED ONION RINGS

(1) About 1 hour before serving, core stem ends of tomatoes; cut tomatoes into 1-inch wedges. Place in a glass bowl.
(2) Separate onion slices into rings and scatter over tomatoes, along with the basil leaves and salt.
(3) Drizzle with olive oil and Balsamic vinegar. Toss lightly and leave at room temperature until serving time.
(4) Garnish with a basil sprig.

INGREDIENTS

4 medium garden ripe tomatoes, about 5 or 6 ounces each
4 thin slices from a medium size red onion
4 large basil leaves, torn into small pieces
salt to taste
2 tablespoons of olive oil
1 tablespoon of balsamic vinegar
sprig of basil
SERVES 4

BROILED TOMATO SLICES
WITH TARRAGON

(1) Core stem ends of tomatoes; cut into half-inch thick slices.
(2) Arrange slices in a baking dish.
(3) Sprinkle a little salt and a little sugar on tomato slices.
(4) Blend crumbs, tarragon, and parsley. Sprinkle over each slice.
(5) Drizzle with olive oil to moisten the crumb mixture.
(6) Broil 4 inches from heat until crumbs are browned and tomatoes are hot.

INGREDIENTS

2 large ripe tomatoes
salt
sugar
1/4 cup of bread crumbs
2 tablespoons of snipped tarragon
2 tablespoons of chopped parsley
olive oil (about 1 teaspoon per tomato slice)

SERVES 3-4

BLACK BEAN SALAD

(1) In a medium bowl, combine the black beans, red onion, cucumber, red pepper, garlic, cilantro, pepper, and cumin seeds.
(2) Add salt to taste.
(3) Cover and chill for a least 3 hours or overnight.
(4) Garnish with cilantro or parsley.

NOTE: This recipe should be made the day before serving as the ingredients should marinate for full flavor. For an interesting variation toss this salad with freshly cooked pasta and serve with a sprinkling of cheddar cheese.

INGREDIENTS

32 ounces of black beans, drained and rinsed
1 cup of minced red onion
1 large cucumber, diced
1 red pepper, diced
2 large cloves of garlic, minced
1/4 cup of chopped cilantro
1 teaspoon of black pepper
1 tablespoon of crushed cumin seeds
salt to taste
sprigs of fresh cilantro or parsley

SERVES 4-6

CAJUN MAYONNAISE

(1) In a large bowl, combine mayonnaise, garlic, cilantro, oregano, black pepper, chili powder, mustard, cumin seed, cayenne pepper, and jalapeno peppers. Cover and chill for at least 4 hours or overnight.

(2) Mound into a serving bowl and garnish with cilantro or parsley.

NOTE: *It is best to make this recipe 3 to 4 days before serving. The longer it sits the better it gets. Serve with Cajun Crab Cakes (see page 23) or add a dollop to a bowl of fish chowder. You can also use this as a spread on crackers or toast triangles.*

INGREDIENTS

1 cup of mayonnaise
4 large cloves of garlic, minced
1/4 cup of minced cilantro leaves
1/4 cup of minced oregano leaves
1 teaspoon of ground black pepper
1 teaspoon of Chili Powder (see Herbal Hint #22, page 5)
1 teaspoon of dried mustard
1 teaspoon of crushed cumin seed
pinch of cayenne pepper
2 jalapeno peppers, cored, and minced
cilantro or parsley, chopped

MAKES 1 CUP

GARDEN VEGETABLE SALAD

(1) Boil carrots for 5 minutes, drain and cool.
(2) Boil string beans for 7 minutes, drain and cool.
(3) In a medium bowl, combine carrots, string beans, corn, red peppers, zucchini, cucumber, squash, celery, scallion, basil, and parsley.
(4) Add oil, both vinegars, pepper and salt to taste. Combine well.
(5) Line a large glass bowl or individual bowls with the lettuce leaves.
(6) Spoon the salad into the bowls and garnish with basil, parsley, or garlic chive blossoms.

NOTE: *Keep the color varied and remember that this can be easily doubled or tripled for a* big party. *Serve as an appetizer or side dish with* meats, *poultry, or fish, cold or at room temperature. To stretch it you might want to add some boiled, diced potatoes or rice.*

INGREDIENTS

1 cup of carrots
1 cup of string beans, cut into 2-inch pieces
1 cup of cooked corn kernels
1 cup of diced red peppers
1/2 cup of diced zucchini
1/2 cup of diced cucumber
1/2 cup of diced yellow squash
1/2 cup of diced celery
1/2 cup of diced scallion, top included
1/4 cup of minced basil leaves
1/4 cup of minced flat leaf parsley
1/3 cup of olive oil
2 tablespoons of balsamic vinegar
2 tablespoons of red wine vinegar
1 teaspoon of black pepper
salt to taste
1 head red leaf or Boston lettuce
basil leaves, flat leaf parsley, or garlic chive blossoms

SERVES 4-6

HERB GARDEN POTATO SALAD

(1) Boil the potatoes in their skins and peel.
(2) Cut the potatoes into eighths and place in a large bowl.
(3) Add the garlic, garlic chives, rosemary, thyme, tarragon, lemon verbena, and parsley. Combine well.
(4) Add the olive oil, both vinegars, salt, black pepper, and cayenne to your taste. Combine again and reseason as your taste requires.
(5) Transfer to a serving bowl and garnish with chive blossoms, nasturtiums, or sprigs of parsley.

NOTE: *Make this recipe with whatever herbs are fresh in the garden. Serve warm, as soon as the salad is made or chilled, a day or two later. This salad will hold 3 to 4 days in the refrigerator.*

INGREDIENTS

12 medium red skin or Russet potatoes
2 cloves of garlic, minced
3 tablespoons of minced garlic chives
1 tablespoon of rosemary needles, minced
1 tablespoon of thyme leaves
1 teaspoon of minced tarragon
1 tablespoon of minced lemon verbena
2 tablespoons of minced flat leaf parsley
1/3 cup of olive oil
2 tablespoons of balsamic vinegar
2 tablespoons of red wine or white wine vinegar
2 teaspoons of salt
1 tablespoon of freshly ground pepper
cayenne pepper
chive blossoms, nasturtiums, or sprigs of parsley

SERVES 4-6

ORANGE AND RED ONION SALAD

(1) Rinse and coarsely chop the arugula, discarding the roots.
(2) Spread the arugula over the entire surface of a serving platter.
(3) Prepare oranges by peeling down to the flesh and slicing into 1/4-inch circles. Remove the core and pits with a sharp knife.
(4) Peel and slice onions into 1/4-inch circles leaving the slices whole.
(5) Alternate and overlap the orange slices and onion slices on top of the arugula forming a circle or a line down the center of the plate, depending on the shape of the platter.
(6) Sprinkle the olives on top along with the oil and vinegar.
(7) Add the oregano leaves, lots of freshly ground pepper, and garnish with the rigani.
(8) Serve chilled or at room temperature.

INGREDIENTS

2 bunches of arugula (chopped this should equal about 4 cups)
4 naval or blood oranges
2 medium red onions
1/2 cup of oil cured black olives
1/4 cup of olive oil
1/8 cup of red wine vinegar
2 tablespoons of minced oregano leaves
pepper to taste
8 rigani (oregano) blossoms

NOTE: *This sparkling and refreshing salad can be served as an appetizer or as a palate refresher between courses. Rigani is the crunchy oregano flower blossom. To serve individually, portion into separate salad dishes.*

SERVES 4

HOT HERB-GARLIC BREAD

Preheat oven to 400° F.

(1) Cut bread diagonally into 1-inch slices, leaving each slice attached at the bottom of the loaf.
(2) Blend soft butter, herbs, and garlic thoroughly.
(3) Lay a piece of foil large enough to wrap completely around loaf on your cutting board or counter. Place loaf in center of foil.
(4) Using a brush or small spatula, spread butter mixture on both sides of each slice, holding the slices apart with one hand and spreading with the other.
(5) Shape foil around loaf in a boat fashion, twisting the ends and leaving the top open. Brush any remaining butter on top and sprinkle with parmesan cheese.
(6) Bake for 10 minutes. Serve hot.

INGREDIENTS

14-inch loaf crusty Italian bread
1/2 cup of soft butter
2 teaspoons of minced parsley
2 teaspoons of finely snipped dillweed
2 teaspoons of chopped oregano
1 clove of garlic, finely minced or squeezed through a garlic press
Parmesan cheese, grated

NOTE: *This bread can be prepared ahead up to step (5). It freezes exceptionally well. Wrap the foil completely around loaf. Open the top when bread is defrosted and ready to be baked. Keep one in the freezer ready to be heated when you need it in a hurry.*

SERVES 4

JALAPENO PEPPER, BUTTERMILK
MADELEINES

Preheat oven to 425° F.

(1) Coat the madeleine pans with cooking shortening.
(2) In a large bowl, combine cornmeal, flour, sugar, baking soda, salt and pepper.
(3) In a small bowl, combine buttermilk, melted butter, jalapenos, chives, and egg. Add to dry ingredients and mix only until moistened.
(4) Spread one tablespoon of batter into each madeleine form. Bake 9-11 minutes or until golden brown. Serve warm.

NOTE: *It seems a shame to use madeleine pans only for dessert madeleines. These bake in 9 or 10 minutes, have great flavor, look appealing and are easy to unmold.*

INGREDIENTS

shortening to coat pan
1 cup of yellow cornmeal
1 cup of unbleached all-purpose flour
2 tablespoons of sugar
1 teaspoon of baking soda
1/2 teaspoon of salt
3/4 teaspoon of freshly ground pepper
1 1/2 cups of buttermilk
1/4 cup of butter, melted
1/4 cup of finely diced jalapeno peppers
2 tablespoons of minced chives
1 egg or 2 egg whites, beaten

MAKES 3 1/2 DOZEN

NO KNEAD

HERB CASSEROLE BREAD

(1) In a large mixing bowl, combine first nine ingredients.
(2) Heat water, milk, and oil over low heat until warm, (100-110° F.)
(3) Add warm liquid to the flour mixture, then the egg. Mix at low speed on electric mixer until moistened, then beat 3 minutes at medium speed.
(4) Gradually stir in white flour, just enough to form a stiff batter.
(5) Cover dough with a clean cloth; allow to rise in a warm place until doubled in bulk, about 50 minutes.
(6) Stir down batter with a wooden spoon.
(7) Spoon batter into two well-greased 1-quart glass casseroles or one 2-quart casserole.

Preheat oven to 375° F.

(8) Let rise for 15 minutes.
(9) Bake for 40 minutes or until loaf sounds hollow when tapped on the top. Remove bread from casserole; cool on a rack.

INGREDIENTS

1 1/2 cups of whole wheat flour
1/4 cup of brown sugar
2 tablespoons of finely chopped fresh onion
1 clove of garlic, finely minced or put through a garlic press
1 1/2 teaspoons of salt
2 packages of active dry yeast
1 teaspoon of chopped marjoram
1 teaspoon of chopped oregano
1 teaspoon of chopped basil
1/2 cup of water
1 cup of low-fat milk
1/4 cup of vegetable oil
1 egg at room temperature
2 1/2 to 3 cups of unbleached all-purpose flour

MAKES 1 LARGE OR 2 SMALL LOAVES

ROSEMARY FEATHER BISCUITS

Preheat oven to 450° F.

(1) Sift together the flour, baking soda and salt.
(2) Cut in butter pieces with a fork or pastry blender until the mixture resembles small peas.
(3) Combine vinegar, milk, and rosemary; add to flour mixture. Mix only until the flour is moistened.
(4) Gather dough together into a ball and knead lightly 3 or 4 times.
(5) Roll or pat out the dough until it is 1/2-inch thick.
(6) Cut the dough into mounds with a biscuit cutter dipped in flour.
(7) Bake on ungreased baking sheet for 10-12 minutes. Serve hot!

INGREDIENTS

2 cups of all-purpose flour
1 teaspoon of baking soda
1/2 teaspoon of salt
1/4 cup of cold butter cut into small pieces
1/4 cup of white vinegar
1/2 cup of milk
1 tablespoon of snipped rosemary needles

NOTE: *These biscuits are feathery light and are particularly good at breakfast or at tea time.*

MAKES 6-8 2 1/2-INCH BISCUITS

THYME AND ONION FLATBREAD

Preheat oven to 350° F.

(1) On a floured pastry board, roll the dough into a 14x10-inch rectangle.
(2) Lay the dough on a cookie sheet and allow to rest for about 10 minutes.
(3) In a small bowl, combine the oil, onion, and thyme.
(4) Spread the onion mixture over the bread right to the edges.
(5) Press the onions down into the dough. Sprinkle with desired amount of salt and pepper.
(6) Cover lightly with a dish towel and allow to rise in a warm place for 30 minutes.
(7) Bake for 30 to 40 minutes or until top is golden.
(8) Remove from oven and cool on a rack.
(9) Cut into 4-inch squares or break apart by hand.

INGREDIENTS

1/2 cup of flour for pastry board
1 pound of bread dough
1/3 cup of olive oil
1 cup of minced onion
1/8 cup of fresh thyme leaves
salt
freshly ground pepper

NOTE: *Serve as part of a bread basket, with salad and a main course, or as a snack. If using the following day, reheat for 10 minutes before serving.*

MAKES ABOUT 12 PIECES

SAGE AND RAISIN SCONES

Preheat oven to 375° F.

(1) In a medium bowl, combine the flour, 1/4 cup of sugar, baking powder, baking soda, salt, and sage.
(2) Cut in the butter pieces with a fork or pastry blender until the mixture resembles coarse meal.
(3) With a fork stir in the buttermilk just to combine.
(4) Sprinkle a board with a bit of flour and turn the dough onto the board. Knead in the raisins.
(5) Flour your hands and press the dough down to form a rectangle about 1/2-inch thick.
(6) With a sharp knife or a square or round cookie cutter, cut out 8 to 10 scones, re-kneading the scraps to make more.
(7) Transfer to a cookie sheet leaving at least 1-inch between each scone.
(8) Bake for 10 minutes.
(9) While the scones are baking combine the milk, cinnamon, and confectioners' sugar.
(10) Brush the milk mixture on each scone and bake for 5 more minutes or until they are golden on top.
(11) Cool on a rack and serve warm for breakfast or with afternoon tea accompanied by sweet butter, clotted cream, or Gingery Cranberry Relish (see page 46).

NOTE: *Wrap these scones in a napkin and bring them as a house gift with homemade orange marmalade or Gingery Cranberry Relish.*

❧ INGREDIENTS

3 cups of flour plus extra for rolling dough
1/4 cup of sugar
2 1/2 teaspoons of baking powder
1/4 teaspoon of baking soda
1/4 teaspoon of salt
1/8 cup of minced fresh sage leaves
12 tablespoons of cold sweet butter, cut into small pieces
1 cup of buttermilk
1/8 cup of flour for pressing down dough
2/3 cup of raisins
1 tablespoon of milk
1 teaspoon of cinnamon
3 tablespoons of confectioners' sugar

MAKES 8-10 SCONES

WHOLE WHEAT
HERB SEED CRACKERS

Preheat oven to 375° F.

(1) Stir the two flours, sesame seeds, salt, and celery seed.
(2) Make a well in the center and pour in the oil. Stir.
(3) Gradually add water, stirring as you add, until the dough holds together in a ball.
(4) Divide ball in half; roll out on a cutting board to a 1/16-inch thickness.
(5) Cut with a small round, scalloped cookie cutter. You may cut into squares or diamonds with a scalloped pastry wheel.
(6) Place dough on ungreased cookie sheets, brush with egg white; sprinkle with topping.
(7) Bake for 15 minutes. Crackers should be nicely browned on the bottom.
(8) Store in a tin. Use with spreads and dips such as those found in this book.

INGREDIENTS

Crackers

1 1/2 cups of whole wheat flour
1/4 cup of all-purpose flour
1/4 cup of sesame seeds, toasted then whirred in the spice mill or blender
3/4 teaspoon of salt
1 teaspoon of celery seed
1/3 cup of canola or safflower oil
1/2 cup of (approximately) water
Egg substitute or lightly whipped egg white for brushing tops

Topping (mix together)

1 teaspoon each of caraway seeds and poppy seeds, toasted
1 teaspoon of coarse salt (less, if desired)

NOTE: *These crackers are a bit chewy. Roll them as thin as possible to make them more crisp.*

MAKES 5 DOZEN CRACKERS

BAY LEAF FLAVORED

CUSTARD SAUCE

(1) Bring water to boil in the bottom of a double boiler.

(2) In a small pan, add bay leaves to the milk and heat until milk is scalded.

(3) In a small bowl, combine the eggs, sugar, and salt.

(4) Whisk scalded milk mixture gradually into the egg mixture. Pour into top of the double boiler set over the boiling water.

(5) Cook, whisking, until the mixture thickens and coats a metal spoon. Remove from heat and pour custard into a glass bowl to cool.

(6) Remove bay leaves before serving over fresh fruit. Garnish, if desired, with a scented geranium leaf or a strip of orange rind, knotted.

INGREDIENTS

1 1/3 cups of low-fat milk
3 fresh bay leaves, torn in half
2 whole eggs
1 tablespoon of sugar
pinch of salt
scented geranium leaf or strip of orange rind, knotted

NOTE: *Try this sauce over fresh blueberries or peeled sliced ripe peaches!*

NOTE: *1/2 cup of egg substitute can replace 2 whole eggs. The custard will take longer to thicken.*

SERVES 4

APPLE BLUEBERRY HERB PIE

Preheat oven to 350° F.

To Prepare Crust:

(1) In a medium bowl, cut the butter into the flour with a fork or pastry blender until the mixture resembles a coarse meal.

(2) Make a well in the center of the dough and add the egg yolk and 2 tablespoons of water.

(3) With a fork, stir until a ball forms using more water if necessary.

(4) Wrap the ball in wax paper and chill 20 minutes or until ready to roll out.

To Prepare Filling:

(5) Combine the apples, blueberries, sugar, mint, thyme, flour or tapioca, and cinnamon in a large bowl and set aside for at least 15 minutes.

(6) On a lightly floured board, roll out half to two thirds of the dough to fit a 9-inch pie dish with a 1/2-inch overlapping edge.

(7) Trim and crimp the edges.

(8) Add the pie filling, mounding in the center.

(9) Roll out the remaining dough into a 10-inch circle and with a serrated edged cutter or a sharp knife cut out six 10-inch long strips of dough.

(10) Lattice the strips onto the top of the filling and crimp the edges to seal.

(11) Fit a sheet of tin foil in a baking tray and place the pie on top.

(12) Bake in the center of the preheated oven until filling is bubbly and crust is golden, about 1 to 1 1/2 hours. If crust starts to brown too quickly place a sheet of tin foil over the top until it is done.

(13) Remove from the oven and cool on a rack. While pie is still hot, sprinkle on some of the thyme and mint. The hot pie will absorb the flavor of the herbs.

NOTE: *Serve with ice cream or slightly whipped heavy cream, unsweetened.*

INGREDIENTS

Crust:

2 cups of flour
10 tablespoons of cold, sweet butter, cut into small pieces
1 egg yolk
4 tablespoons of ice water
extra flour for rolling out dough

Filling:

2 cups of peeled, cored, sliced apples
2 cups of blueberries, rinsed
3/4 cup of sugar
2 tablespoons of minced mint
1 teaspoon of whole thyme leaves
3 tablespoons of flour or quick cooking tapioca grains
2 teaspoons of cinnamon
fresh mint
thyme leaves

SERVES 8

BREAD PUDDING
WITH HERBS AND FRUIT

Preheat oven to 375° F.

(1) Prepare a large 3-inch deep casserole dish by coating with the butter. Set aside.
(2) Place the bread in a large bowl and set aside.
(3) In a medium bowl, beat the milk, sugar, and eggs to a froth. Add the lemon rind, oregano, thyme, mint, and cayenne pepper. Combine well.
(4) Gradually add the milk mixture to the bread and combine so that all the bread is soaked. Allow to sit about 15 minutes.
(5) Spread the apples on the bottom of the casserole and add the bread mixture on top.
(6) Sprinkle on the berries and nectarines pressing them down into the bread with a fork. Sprinkle with the brown sugar.
(7) Bake for 45 minutes or until puffed and golden.
(8) Remove from oven and place on a rack to cool slightly.
(9) To serve, spoon some of the pudding onto dessert dishes and add a serving of ice cream. Garnish with herbs and extra fruit.

NOTE: *This is best when served on the warm side. To serve the following day, cover and keep chilled. Bring to room temperature and warm just before serving. Much of the flavor of this recipe comes from the bread. It is important to try and use either homemade bread or good quality bakery French or Italian bread. Most natives of New Orleans will tell you that you can only make good bread pudding with bread from New Orleans.*

INGREDIENTS

2 tablespoons of sweet butter, softened
6 cups of day-old hard crust bread, broken into small chunks
4 cups of milk, regular or low fat
1/2 cup of sugar
3 large eggs
1 tablespoon of grated lemon zest
1 tablespoon of oregano leaves, minced
1 tablespoon of thyme leaves
1 tablespoon of mint leaves, minced
1 pinch cayenne pepper
1 cup of peeled, cored, diced apples
1 cup of blueberries or raspberries
1 cup of diced nectarine (optional)
1/2 cup of brown sugar
1 pint vanilla or chocolate ice cream (optional)
extra fruit and herbs

SERVES 6

CORIANDER AND APRICOT
CAKE

Preheat oven to 350° F.

(1) Coat a 10-inch springform tube pan with butter. Set aside.
(2) In a small bowl, combine the topping ingredients. Set aside.
(3) In another small bowl, sift together the flour, baking powder, and salt.
(4) Stir in the coriander and walnuts. Set aside.
(5) In a mixer or by hand, cream the butter with the sugar until smooth. Add the eggs, and beat to a pale yellow mixture.
(6) Beat the flour mixture into the butter alternately with the sour cream and then beat in the vanilla extract.
(7) With a spoon or spatula swirl in the apricot preserve.
(8) Spoon half the batter into the prepared pan. Sprinkle on one half of the topping. Add the rest of the batter and the remaining topping.
(9) Bake for 45 minutes to 1 hour or until a tester comes out clean.
(10) Cool on a rack then unmold.
(11) Invert cake onto a serving platter and sprinkle with powdered sugar just before serving.

NOTE: *Coriander seeds are a wonderful result of growing cilantro. Looking for a way to use my crop of seeds, I came up with this delicious cake. It holds well for days and is better the day after it is baked as it becomes permeated with the flavor of coriander. -MKP*

INGREDIENTS

1 1/2 tablespoons of soft butter for pan

Topping:
1/2 cup of sugar
1/2 cup of coarsely chopped walnuts
2 teaspoons of cinnamon

Batter:
2 cups of flour
1 1/2 teaspoons of baking powder
1/4 teaspoon of salt
1 tablespoon of crushed coriander seeds
1/2 cup of finely chopped walnuts
10 tablespoons of soft butter
1 cup of sugar
2 eggs
1 cup of sour cream
1 teaspoon of vanilla extract
1/2 cup of apricot preserve mixed with 1 tablespoon of water
powdered sugar

SERVES 8-10

SUMMER FRUIT COMPOTE
WITH LEMON BALM AND MINT

(1) Combine the fruit, lemon balm, mint, liqueur or vanilla, and sugar.
(2) Let this mixture marinate for an hour in the refrigerator.
(3) Serve chilled with fresh mint sprigs.

INGREDIENTS

1 cup of blueberries, washed and drained
2 ripe peaches (or nectarines), peeled and sliced
1 cup of strawberries, washed, drained, and halved
1/4 of a cantaloupe, seeded, peeled, and cut into half-inch cubes
1/2 cup of cherries, pitted, and halved
2 tablespoons of lemon balm leaves, washed, dried, and chopped
2 tablespoons of mint leaves, washed, dried, and chopped
1 or 2 tablespoons of strawberry liqueur or 1 teaspoon of vanilla extract
2 teaspoons of sugar
mint sprigs

SERVES 4-6

WINTER FRUIT COMPOTE WITH MINT

(1) Prepare the fruit, except for the banana.
(2) Combine the fruit in a bowl. Add mint flakes, orange peel, and liqueur.
(3) Chill.
(4) When ready to serve, peel, slice, and add banana. Mix gently.

INGREDIENTS

2 kiwi fruit, peeled and diced or sliced
1 cup of red or green seedless grapes, washed, and halved
1 golden delicious apple, peeled, quartered, cored, and diced
1 orange, peeled, sliced, and slices cut in quarters
11 ounces of mandarin orange sections, with juice
1 tablespoon of dried mint flakes
1 teaspoon of freshly grated orange peel
1 tablespoon of orange liqueur (optional)
1 banana

SERVES 4-6

PEACH KUCHEN
WITH FRESH HERBS

(1) Sift together the flour, baking powder, salt, and sugar.
(2) Cut in the butter with a fork or pastry blender until the mixture resembles coarse meal.
(3) Whip the egg lightly and add the milk. Blend into flour mixture with a fork.
(4) Gather dough into a ball, wrap in wax paper, and chill for several hours.

Preheat oven to 400° F.

(5) Cut dough in half and oil a 12-inch pizza pan. Pat dough into pan, making sure it is evenly distributed from center to edges. It should be a thin layer of dough. At first it may seem as if there isn't enough dough, but keep pressing from center out until entire pan is covered.
(6) Combine cinnamon and sugar.
(7) Sprinkle half of the thyme leaves over the dough. Arrange fruit slices symmetrically around pan, pressing lightly into dough. Sprinkle with remaining thyme leaves and the cinnamon mixture.
(8) Bake for 25-30 minutes until crust is brown and fruit is bubbling.
(9) While kuchen is baking, melt 1/4 cup of currant jelly over low heat.
(10) When the kuchen is done, remove from oven and stand on a cooling rack. Carefully brush the melted jelly over the fruit slices.
(11) Cut the kuchen into wedges and serve it warm with freshly whipped cream flavored with vanilla and sugar.

For one Apple Kuchen: Substitute 4 or 5 golden delicious apples for the peaches. The apples should be peeled, quartered, cored, and sliced into 1/4-inch pieces. Also substitute 1/4 cup of freshly chopped sage for the thyme.

NOTE: The dough recipe is enough for two kuchens. Freeze half for future use if desired. Fruit topping quantities are for one kuchen.

NOTE: The German word "kuchen" brings to mind all kinds of delicious fruit topped cakes that my grandmother baked all summer long.
-JWM

INGREDIENTS

2 1/4 cups of all-purpose flour
1 1/2 teaspoons of baking powder
1/2 teaspoon of salt
1/2 cup of sugar
3/4 cup of butter
1 egg
1/3 cup of milk
4 or 5 large peaches, peeled, and sliced into 1/2-inch slices
1/4 cup of fresh thyme leaves
1/4 teaspoons of cinnamon
2 tablespoons of sugar
1/4 cup of currant jelly for glaze

SERVES 8

CHUCK'S BEST BLOODY MARY

(1) Blend the tomato juice, Worcestershire sauce, lemon and lime juices, vodka, sherry pepper, and horseradish together in a 1-quart jar.
(2) Chill for 2-3 hours.
(3) Shake and serve over ice.
(4) Garnish with the leafy top of a celery stalk or a sprig of lovage, which has a celery flavor.

INGREDIENTS

23 ounces of tomato juice
1 tablespoon of Worcestershire sauce
2 tablespoons of fresh lemon juice
2 tablespoons of fresh lime juice
8 ounces of vodka
1 tablespoon of Sherry Pepper (below)
1 to 2 tablespoons of freshly grated horseradish root, to taste
celery stalk tops or lovage sprigs

MAKES 1 QUART (SERVES 4)

SHERRY PEPPER

(1) Add the peppers to the sherry.
(2) Recap the bottle and store in a cool, dark place for a couple of weeks or longer.

NOTE: *Be sure to make this recipe ahead of time. Use the sherry pepper to perk up soups, sauces, and Bloody Marys. It keeps indefinitely. Pour some into recycled soy sauce bottles with shaker tops for easy dispensing. If you don't have the sherry pepper, add a tablespoon of dry sherry and 1/4 teaspoon of hot pepper flakes to the drink.*

INGREDIENTS

1 fifth of inexpensive dry sherry
10 dried hot peppers

MAKES 1 FIFTH GALLON

HOT MINTED CHOCOLATE

(1) In a medium saucepan, whisk together the cocoa, sugar, 3 mint sprigs, salt, and water. Allow to steep for 30 minutes.
(2) Place over medium heat, and gradually add the milk, stirring constantly. Simmer over low heat for about 10 minutes, stirring frequently.
(3) Discard the mint leaves and pour into cups.
(4) Garnish with fresh sprigs of mint and serve.

NOTE: *Pour this over a few ice cubes in a tall glass. It leaves you feeling wonderfully refreshed and energized.*

INGREDIENTS

1/4 cup of cocoa
4 tablespoons of sugar
3 sprigs of fresh mint
pinch of salt
1/4 cup of water
2 1/4 cups of milk
sprigs of mint

SERVES 4

HOT SPICED APPLE CIDER

(1) Tie allspice and cloves in a little cheesecloth packet or place in a small tea caddy.

(2) In a saucepan, bring apple cider, water, tea bags, orange slices, cinnamon, and spice packet or tea caddy to a boil. Lower heat and simmer for a few minutes.

(3) With a slotted spoon, remove tea bags, orange slices, and spice packet.

(4) Simmer another 5 minutes and serve hot garnished with fresh slices of orange and lemon.

NOTE: *This delicious punch is also good served cold in the summer with fresh mint or lemon verbena added to each serving.*

INGREDIENTS

5 whole allspice berries
3 whole cloves
1 quart of apple cider
2 cups of water
2 tea bags - look for tea flavored with orange or apple and cinnamon or cranberry-apple
1 small orange with peel, thinly sliced
1 stick of cinnamon
orange slices
lemon slices

SERVES 8

RED RASPBERRY HERBAL SUN TEA

(1) Fill a 1-quart jar with fresh cold water. Add the tea bags and mint sprigs and lemon balm.
(2) Seal the jar and let stand in the hot sun for a few hours.
(3) Remove the tea bags, add the lemonade mix or concentrate, stir or shake and serve over ice garnished with fresh mint sprigs.

NOTE: This elegant tea is made with caffeine free tea, and it is a flavorful beverage for children and adults. There's no boiling of water to make the kitchen hot in summer.

INGREDIENTS

1 quart of fresh cold water
3 regular sized red raspberry caffeine free herb tea bags
4 sprigs of spearmint
4 sprigs of lemon balm
1 teaspoon of powdered lemonade flavor drink mix or 2 tablespoons of frozen lemonade concentrate
mint sprigs

MAKES 1 QUART

RIESLING WITH
WOODRUFF AND FRUIT

(1) Pour wine into a glass jar or pitcher.
(2) Add the woodruff, berries, orange, and lemon slices.
(3) Let this mixture marinate for a few hours.
(4) Serve over ice in a stemmed glass.
(5) Garnish with a sprig of woodruff.
(6) Club soda can be added to make it a spritzer.

NOTE: *This is a refreshing spring or summer wine-based beverage with a unique flavor. Sweet woodruff is the herb used in traditional German May wine. Dried woodruff can be used, so pick your woodruff while it is fresh, dry it, and make this drink any time.*

INGREDIENTS

1 750 ml. bottle Riesling or Rhine wine or other slightly sweet white wine
2 or 3 sprigs of fresh woodruff and blossoms, if blooming
6 fresh strawberries
3 fresh lemon slices
3 fresh orange slices

SERVES 4

INDEX